Hell & Back

Hell & Back

WIFE & MOTHER
DOCTOR & PATIENT
DRAGON SLAYER

Tali Lando Aronoff, MD

ARCHWAY
PUBLISHING

Archway Publishing books may be ordered through booksellers or by contacting:

Archway Publishing
1663 Liberty Drive
Bloomington, IN 47403
www.archwaypublishing.com
1 (888) 242-5904

ISBN: 978-1-4808-6176-3 (sc)
ISBN: 978-1-4808-6175-6 (hc)
ISBN: 978-1-4808-6177-0 (e)

Library of Congress Control Number: 2018904943

Print information available on the last page.

Archway Publishing rev. date: 06/06/2018

To My Mother

For always believing in me, my entire life and for believing in this book even when it was a crude set of ramblings on my laptop. For your endless patience. For the countless hours we spent together re-reading, revising and tightening my story and designing the cover. Thank you. I love you.

To My Precious Girls

For your mature understanding and support when Mommy was busy writing. You are the three reasons I will always put one foot in front of the other.

To Alex

My partner. My rock. For living through it all with me and coming out the other side, then reliving it again in print.

Facebook
https://www.facebook.com/hellandbackbook

@hellandbackbook
#hellandbackbook

Website
www.hellandbackbook.com

Contents

Prologue xiii

SUMMER

When Good Genes Fail 1
Delivering Bad News to Family 10
"Eureka- I Found It" 12
When to Play the C-Card 17
The Butterfly Effect 21
D-Day 25
Doctors Are the Worst Patients 30
I Hate My Jackson-Pratts 34
The Unscratchable Itch 37
I Thought I Had "The Good Cancer" 41
Managing Regret 46
The Pity Face 53

FALL

When Friends Come Out of the Woodwork 57
Insomnia and Netflix 65
Parking Wars 70

"The Dirty Dozen" 75

Bitz-n-Pieces 81

Synagogue Celebrity 85

Tripping in the Sukkah... 88

Super Humans with Super Powers...........................92

Going Bra-less in Public 96

A Boo-boo in My Boobies 99

V for Vendetta 103

Pink Night at the Beauty Bar...............................108

Trouble with the Curve.. 112

Therapists and Sympathy at Every Turn...............116

WINTER

Christmakah 120

Stocking the Fridge...123

Mocking the Grim Reaper 127

Mommy is "Working from Home".........................130

Starbucks.... Where Everybody Knows Your Name 133

The Nanny Dance 137

Being the Doctor and the Patient 141

Broken and Bald 150

Funky Sleeves and Misplaced Belly Buttons.....................156

The Michelangelo of Nipple Tattoos 161

Why Are We Talking About Nipples Again? 166

A Rack Like a Porn Star.......................................169

Putting Humpty Back Together Again 172

Radioactive, Radioactive 175

Sexy GI Jane 179

SPRING AND BEYOND

At What Point do I Technically Become "A Survivor" 184

First Steps 187

The Rise and Fall 189

Deep Ravines and Laser Hair Removal 193

The House that Cancer Built 197

The Funeral 203

What About the Husband? 209

Rotten Eggs 215

Giant Pink Tents 219

The Machine 223

Abdominal Binders and Sexy Lingerie 229

The Devil You Know 236

Road Trip! 243

The Further Redistribution of Fat 251

Wearing Heels Again 259

The Bucket List 263

Afterwards 270

Acknowledgments 272

Endnotes 273

Prologue

Being diagnosed with breast cancer is not unlike getting punched in the stomach by your ninety-year-old grandma. It's absurdly unexpected and shocking. It takes a little while to catch your breath and for that shock to settle into acceptance. When I started writing, I was only beginning the months and months of grueling treatment and, honestly, I had barely come to terms with my diagnosis. I needed an outlet for the dark thoughts in my head during the hours I spent awake at night, tossing and turning and willing it to be morning.

Somehow, those thoughts were often peppered by a funny or ironic incident. Eventually, my whole experience morphed into a coherent tale of living in the space between laughter and despair. Hopefully, this book will allow some women and their loved ones to smile knowingly. Maybe it will provide some comic relief as one wades through all the shitty steps we are forced to endure to get to the other side of this illness. It is intended as a helping guide for what comes next, a peek around the corner so you get less spooked when you face the monster. I wanted to provide all the missing bits of information that doctors often omit.

This manuscript sat on my laptop for two years, unfinished.

Then, about six months ago, my strong and talented former chief resident and friend was diagnosed with Stage 1 breast cancer within a year of delivering twins. She was lost and petrified because she didn't know what to expect. Instead of explaining over the phone, I found myself emailing her weekly installments. She said it helped her to feel more prepared. As humans, we crave connections through common experience, the comfort of hearing someone say, "me too." So, I took out my sadly neglected Mac and finished my story to help her live hers. Clearly, I don't have the magic potion to make it all better and I don't have all the answers, not for me or anyone else. Still, there is always light guiding us even in the blackest of times. I trust that reading this book will provide oases of levity in the deluge of pain. If nothing else, I know it helped me immensely to write it.

My story began in the summer...

SUMMER
When Good Genes Fail

"Begin at the beginning," the King said, very
gravely, *"and go on till you come to the end:
then stop."*
　　　　　--Lewis Carrol, *Alice in Wonderland*

I am a 37-year-old pediatric ENT surgeon. I have spent 11
post-college years getting here if you add medical school (4),
otolaryngology residency (5) and pediatric otolaryngology fellowship (2). There's no way around it: it's a giant chunk of my
life spent in the attainment of a single goal. In recent years,
it's finally begun to feel worth it. I love what I do. I love my
patients (at least most of the time), the anatomy involved and
the surgeries I am privileged to perform. Although it can be
stressful and frustrating, as all jobs are, I believe that either by
fate or happy coincidence, I am meant to be doing this work.

In the two years preceding my diagnosis, I had joined a
superb and respected medical practice and had finally started
earning an adult's salary. Oh, and I'd also popped out my third
daughter in four years. My family felt nearly complete and my
husband and I had moved into a friendly community in lower

Westchester. There, we rented an old-charming-small yellow house while we geared up to build our bigger brand-new one. After a rocky start in my early 20s culminating in an unpleasant divorce (sans kids) to a person who I'd foolishly stayed with for five years, I was now married to a wonderful and loving man, my husband Alex.

Life was starting to shape up quite nicely and I thought I was looking at a few years of smooth sailing. There had been a recent bump in the road when, six months earlier, at 34 weeks gestation with my third child, I found out at a routine obstetric exam that I had severe preeclampsia. I had to emergently deliver my unbaked three-pound daughter, Milla Nadiya Aronoff. She was born beautiful and breathing. After that, Alex and I spent five weeks nervously shuttling back and forth to the Neonatal Intensive Care Unit to visit, hold and feed her. Initially, she was frail and tiny. Though she started on CPAP (assisted breathing) and TPN (intravenous feedings), we brought her home, healthy, one-and-a-half months later at a whopping four pounds.

Following my slightly extended maternity leave, I quickly began to ramp up my practice again. I was finally getting more sleep and trying to calibrate my work/life balance. Overall, I was feeling smug, while secretly constantly crossing my fingers, because while I hate to admit it, I was beginning to believe I could have it all.

I had never been afraid of illness. Longevity is in my bloodlines and I had personally always been healthy, both mentally, aside from some requisite neuroses, and physically. More than that, I had never taken a sick day in my entire training, not for the flu or a GI bug or even throughout two pregnancies, one during residency and one during fellowship. In both gestations, I easily worked full 13-hour days on the Fridays immediately before the Sundays on which I was electively induced to minimize out-of-work downtime. My maternal and paternal grandparents had lived full and healthy lives, dying in their late 80s or early 90s from various non-cancerous causes. I had no reason to fear.

In my very large family, including dozens of great aunts, six aunts, and twenty-two female first cousins, there were no recorded incidents of breast cancer. I did fear many scary things, big and small, as most young mothers do (car accidents, chipped teeth, SIDS, autism, etc.), but not this particular disease. I strongly believed in the power of good genes... which is why I ultimately felt so blindsided.

It all began on Saturday night, July 20th at 8:15 pm. I called my mother to see how my parents' weekend was going. "Something is wrong with Aba," she said immediately. My father, affectionately called by the Hebrew name for father, "Aba," had been in a conversation with a group of friends earlier that day when he experienced word-finding problems. Within 24 hours of that call, I found myself sitting at a computer monitor at Columbia-Presbyterian Hospital staring at the scariest image I could imagine: my father's malignant brain tumor. I had spent five years of residency training at that hospital and hundreds of hours on the other side of the desk, in front of those screens. This was different.

I'll never know why, eight days later at one am, lying in my bed and unable to sleep because of concern over my father's impending craniotomy, I inadvertently brushed my right hand against the left side of my chest. When I did, I felt a distinct, hard mass. In that moment, I knew immediately that a storm was coming.

The following day, I woke up at 6:15 am and went to work in OR 2, my usual operating room at the Maria Fareri Children's Hospital of Westchester Medical Center. I had about seven small cases scheduled, mostly tonsillectomies and ear tubes. When I arrived, I saw Fran, my beloved ENT nurse, and I whispered in her ear,

"I felt a lump."

She and another nurse, Maria, escorted me next door where a female Ob-Gyn surgeon was scrubbing into a big hysterectomy case. After another hushed conversation, I started down the path that would lead to my cancer diagnosis.

At 9:01 am, while my first patient was waking up from general anesthesia, I cold-called Dr. Julian Sanchez, the breast radiologist at Westchester Medical Center. Over the phone, he reassured me that because I was young, had no family history and had just stopped nursing several months prior, the lump was most likely a blocked milk duct (called a galactocele). Despite his optimism, he still encouraged me to come in later that day for an examination and imaging. His presumptive theory was soothing, allowing me to finish my work day with less worry. Unfortunately, his assumption was also very wrong.

At 4 pm, after my cases were finished, I drove to the nearby Bradhurst building. Exiting the elevator, I turned right instead of heading straight, as I usually do, to enter my ENT office. Inside the Breast Imaging Center, Dr. Sanchez waited. He and his staff had graciously agreed to stay late so I could come in after work. We started with a simple ultrasound during which time the technician kept asking me to show her where the lump was located. This part was confusing, even for me as a physician, because the mass was sizable and easily palpable (~2 cm and larger on an MRI). Didn't she feel it? I was very briefly lulled into a false sense of hope that I might have imagined the whole thing. No such luck. Minutes later, I was shepherded across the hall into another room with a large, ominous piece of machinery. Another pretty young technician positioned me for my first mammogram. This is an unpleasant experience that requires you to stand semi-naked on your tiptoes while the machine lifts your pancaked breast into an awkward anti-gravity position. It felt as though my left breast was about to be ripped off.

She repeated the imaging from three different angles. Although I couldn't tell exactly what was happening, I began to suspect there was something bad lurking inside of me, and they wanted to get a better look at it. The technician kept coming into the room to reposition me while smiling nervously. She then returned to her booth to snap the requisite shots. By the time Dr. Sanchez came in the room 10 minutes later, I was already fighting back tears. I have no specific memory of what he told me, but I can still hear the words, *"I'm so sorry."* Apparently, my mammogram was straight out of a textbook on breast cancer imaging 101. He offered me an immediate biopsy. I instantly accepted.

"It may still be carcinoma-in-situ," he offered gently. I understood he was just trying to keep me positive. I called Natalie from the waiting room while the team set up for the core biopsy. She is a breast radiologist and one of my best friends from medical school. It still gives me goosebumps to think about how everything had come full circle in that moment.

During our second year of medical school at Cornell, I underwent a fine needle aspiration of a small benign breast cyst. The physician who performed the procedure was an intense and super intelligent young Russian woman... just like Natalie. When I returned to the Lasdon dormitory that afternoon, I immediately took the elevator one flight up to Natalie's apartment to inform her that I had undoubtedly found her future profession.

The whole class was at a crossroads at that point, anxiously waiting for some divine voice from on high to tell us what specialty we were meant to pursue. Unlike the rest of us, Natalie never seemed stressed about this decision. She figured it would all work itself out eventually. At the time, she was skeptical about my epiphany and, despite my excitement, she seemed to take my advice lightly. Yet, something must have stuck. Either way, a decade later, Natalie had become a well-respected Breast Radiologist at Maimonides Medical Center in Brooklyn. She was now on the phone with me, listening to the panic in my voice.

"Text me the images."

I hung on, shaking in my borrowed bathrobe, while she absorbed what she saw.

"I'm not going to sugar coat it. It's cancer and it's invasive and we're going to have to deal with it... together."

Sometimes, hearing the unbridled truth is calming. There is no waiting and hoping for better news. I just moved right on to dealing with it. I dried my tears and got dressed. I thanked everyone politely and drove myself home. I called Alex from the car and started with something like,

"Baby, I know this will be hard to believe but..."

Later that night while I sat at my kitchen table, sobbing into the phone, Natalie walked me step by step through the process ahead. She eased me into my new reality in a way no one else could ever have done. Natalie was there, unhappily yet honestly, delivering every piece of bad news from that moment forward. It was Natalie who subsequently re-did the ultrasound of my breast and armpit, finding the one otherwise unsuspicious lymph node that "just didn't look quite right." And it was Natalie who had to tell me that her biopsy proved the nasty cat was out of the bag: cancer had officially spread to my lymph nodes. She was and still is amazing to me and I wish everyone could have a Natalie like mine to cushion the blow.

The following day, I sat with my mother and brothers in the neurosurgical waiting room at Columbia Presbyterian, biting my nails and waiting for any word on my father's post-operative condition. In the hallway by the elevators, I had already told my three brothers and two of my sisters-in-law about the development in my health. I had not told my mother, not yet. As much as I may have needed her, I felt there was only so much one woman could absorb. She deserved to deal with one major life crisis at a time. When the surgeon smiled and said everything had gone as well as expected, I thanked God for going easy on us that day. As it turns out, He was still holding out on me.

The next set of events happened so quickly that I never had time to process them. In hindsight, I wonder if all the shortcuts I took due to my medical connections ultimately hurt me. Most people would argue that the faster you cut the tumor out, the better. I guess at this point none of it matters. However, the speed at which my surgical planning evolved robbed me of the chance to grieve. I had to focus entirely on action-oriented behaviors. There was too much to get done.

Within a week, I had completed a breast MRI, a whole-body PET scan, and a brain MRI, as well as genetic testing. Natalie nimbly fast-tracked the entire process. In those early days, she whisked me out of the Maimonides waiting room day after day. I hardly felt like a patient. Instead of sitting with everyone else, I sat in a back corner of her dim office drinking coffee and eating doughnuts while she interpreted the images of other women's breasts that were displayed on her large computer screen.

By Wednesday, only two days after my diagnosis, Natalie had set up an informal consultation with Dr. Patrick Borgen, the amazing breast oncologic surgeon who would ultimately perform my surgery. He is the Chairman of the Department of Surgery of Maimonides Medical Center in Brooklyn, the Chief of Breast Service in the Department of Surgery and Co-Director of the Breast Disease Management team at Memorial Sloan-Kettering in New York City. He also rides a motorcycle and plays in a band. Natalie trusted him without reservation, so I didn't hold those last two facts against him.

Dr. Borgen discussed my various options which theoretically included lumpectomy with radiation, unilateral or bilateral mastectomy. Without having any clear idea of what it would entail, I instinctively decided to go with the whole enchilada: bilateral mastectomy, no holds barred. I was too young to spend the rest of my life waiting for the other shoe to drop. Dr. Borgen patted me on the back.

"Good girl," he said.

In the past, I might have taken offense to this paternalistic gesture. That day, I was comforted. I didn't just appreciate his approval, I needed it. In his eyes, I saw something more than empathy. I saw genuine sadness as he outlined the details of my surgery as if he were telling his own daughter. Afterwards, I met with Dr. Gayle, a superb plastic surgeon. I had met him once before at a private graduation dinner in an exclusive restaurant in downtown Manhattan. He would later take charge of my breast reconstruction.

For the rest of that week, I ran around New York City obtaining the requisite second and third opinions. I was lucky to get expedited appointments. In the end, after appropriate due diligence, I came back to Drs. Borgen and Gayle. With them, I knew I had my personal surgical "A" team. I was offered a surgery date only nine days later and I took it. The tumor had already infiltrated at least one of my lymph nodes. God knows I didn't want to give this bastard a chance to spread any further.

Delivering Bad News to Family

Sitting your parents down at their kitchen table to tell them that you, their only daughter, their prized, cherished doctor-daughter, have breast cancer is never an easy conversation. That level of difficulty is compounded when the conversation occurs one week after your pillar-of-the-community father had his own neurosurgery to remove a glioblastoma, an incurable brain tumor. But, I had avoided the conversation for as long as possible. I had even contemplated not telling them at all. My middle brother, Dov, had forcefully and convincingly asserted that this was unfair and belittling to them as parents. It was 9 o'clock, the night before my bilateral mastectomy with axillary node dissection.

"Mom, Aba. I have something to tell you. It's bad but everything is going to be ok."

As my parents searched my eyes for a clue as to what was coming, I tried to look calm. I provided them with just the facts, sparing them the gravity of my emotions. At that point, the physician in me was still highly functional, having just navigated the entire family back from the brink after my father's crushing diagnosis. When I finished speaking, their response was like that of my husband. They looked at me almost vacantly, a mixed expression of disbelief, denial and an immediate decision not to cry.

I continued to fill the silence with detailed explanations. I tried to make it all sound ordinary. It had been caught early and was likely to be resolved with surgery, and there was only a 50 percent chance I'd require chemotherapy, blah, blah blah... I emphasized the favorable tumor genetics: Estrogen/Progesterone receptor positive/Her-2 Neu negative, which is apparently everything you want in a breast tumor. More importantly, my other studies, with exception of the single lymph node biopsy, were negative for tumor spread. This was the truth, as I knew it at that point, and they seemed to buy into my façade of strength, quickly resolving to mirror it.

I wasn't about to lift the veil and reveal my true fear.

"Eureka- I Found It"

Despite common misconception, most cases of breast cancer are not caused by inherited genetic factors. Most cancers are associated with mutations in breast cells that are acquired during a person's lifetime. They do not typically cluster in families. Nonetheless, a genetic evaluation is a routine part of the workup for breast cancer, particularly in young women. In hereditary breast cancer, the way the cancer is inherited is based on the gene involved. Mutations in the BRCA1 and BRCA2 genes are inherited in an autosomal dominant pattern, which means one copy of the altered gene in each cell is enough to increase the person's risk of developing cancer. The BRCA genes are classified as "high penetrance" because they are associated with a high risk of developing breast cancer and ovarian cancer, as well as other types of cancer. This has serious implications for the women with BRCA+ breast cancer and their children.

First, it means that a prophylactic bilateral oophorectomy (surgical removal of the ovaries) will likely be recommended by the age of 40 to reduce the risk of also developing ovarian cancer. Even scarier, every child of a BRCA+ parent has a 50 percent chance of inheriting the gene. While minors are not typically tested, the challenge of deciding when they are mature enough to be told about their risk is immense. For me, the idea of having passed on a faulty gene with a high probability of eventually causing breast cancer in my daughters was more frightening than any other reality.

At the Maimonides Breast Cancer Center, the waiting area for genetic counseling is just beyond the fancy main waiting room with a self-playing piano. It is located off a little hallway with two folding chairs immediately adjacent to the coffeemaker. Sitting there, I felt like Dorothy awaiting my fate before the great and powerful Oz. When the door eventually opened, a woman who didn't look a day over twenty-five was sitting behind the large desk. She handed me some pamphlets about genetic testing for breast cancer. Thankfully, she paid me the courtesy of skipping over the genetics lecture.

"I'm assuming you remember how all this stuff works. Right?"

I dug deep into my knowledge bank from the second year of medical school.

"Yup. I'm good."

She was all smiles and cheerfulness as we sat down to gather my family history. I started out confidently detailing the extent of my family tree, in which the diagnosis of breast cancer was impressively absent. I was convinced my risk of a germline mutation (genetic mutations that are present in all the body's cells) was extremely low. This cancer was a fluke, accidental and not coded in my DNA. I was sure of it. She perused my paperwork and glanced up with an eyebrow raised.

"So, your father was recently diagnosed with brain cancer, correct?"

"Well, yes. That was another stroke of really bad luck."

"Mmmm. Interesting."

We sat in silence while she tried to access some information stored deep in her brain. Suddenly, after a long pause, she burst out,

"Li-Fraumeni Syndrome!"

"Excuse me?"

She was so excited. She reminded me of Archimedes running naked through the streets screaming, "Eureka- I found it" after he'd noticed the rising water level in his bathtub.

"Li-Fraumeni Syndrome. That could be the genetic connection between you and your father's cancers."

Several nasty genetic syndromes are associated with a significantly increased risk of breast cancer. Li-Fraumeni syndrome is a rare disease in which patients are predisposed to cancer. The Li-Fraumeni cancer spectrum is broad and includes family members with premenopausal breast cancer (check), brain tumors (check) and other cancers. It is a terrible diagnosis and definitely NOT something you want to have. I felt like she should have looked a little less enthusiastic.

"Wait, how old was your father when he was diagnosed?"

"Seventy. It was only a few weeks ago."

"I take it back, probably doesn't meet the criterion then. More likely just two random cancers in one family. Would have been interesting though."

Seriously? For whom?

To my extreme relief, all the bloodwork eventually came back negative for any known heritable breast cancer mutations. I went back to thinking it was just chance, mixed with some potential environmental factors and I was soothed. Despite everything, I felt like I was finally catching a break. Also, I had a conclusive answer to the pressing question on everyone's mind.

*"Do you have **THE** gene?"*

In my Jewish community, asking whether I had the BRCA gene was as casual as asking if I had any extra milk in my fridge. Now I had an appropriate response.

*"No, I don't have **THE** gene..."*

I sure as hell have something.

About six months later, Dr. Miki Hertz, a very close medical school friend, invited me to a BBQ at her house in Rosalyn, Long Island. An Israeli oncologist friend of her mother's, a woman in her mid-fifties, had also been invited. She was a typical Sabra, thorny and tough on the outside yet, in light of her chosen profession, presumably soft and sensitive on the inside. I thought it was a nice opportunity to pick her brain. Miki was excited to make the connection. Naturally, we fell into a conversation about our mutual interest, breast cancer. I updated her on the specifics of my diagnosis and she asked about my genetic work-up. I smiled, watching my girls whiz by up the stairs.

"It was all negative, which was a huge relief, as you can imagine."

I didn't tell her how stressed I had been, waiting for the results. Every time I gave my girls their baths, I couldn't stop looking at their adorable little nipples and thinking of them as ticking time bombs that I needed to defuse. I didn't tell her about the sleepless nights in which I crept into their bedroom, tortured by the price I might pay for having three lovely girls... six potential breasts to harbor cancer.

She paused on the landing, cocking her head to the side.

"That's great. I'm glad to hear it."

Then she laid it on me like a big fat turd.

*"Well, there's always new research and discovery in the field of cancer genetics. So, you are really only negative insofar as the genes we **currently** know about!!!!"*

When to Play the C-Card

My beautiful friend Avital Harari is a tough, talented endocrine surgeon in LA. Avital had loyally stuck by me through several life-changing events: divorce from my first husband during residency, a tumultuous dating career during my year of singledom in NYC, the courtship and marriage to Alex and the pregnancy and birth of my first daughter, Juliette. In short, I owed this girl. When I realized that I had scheduled my bilateral mastectomy for Tuesday, August 13th, I didn't have the guts to cancel my flight to LA for her bachelorette party. The party was a week before the wedding, which now I couldn't attend. My two other amazing physician friends were gathering from Texas and Arizona and we had all planned to have our flights arrive at LAX at the same time. I *had* to be there.

Within an hour of landing, the four of us, Avital, Caroline, Essi and I, had connected via text. After three successful terminal pick-ups, we were all piled into Avital's car. Bubbling with excitement at our reunion, we headed off for some fresh Cali coffee and scones. Avital wandered outside to call her fiancé, Ron, a handsome entertainment lawyer working at a flashy LA firm. As soon as she walked out of earshot, I welled up with tears and blurted out my announcement to the other girls.

"I have fucking cancer."

Within seconds, there wasn't a dry eye in the bunch. Even though I knew she'd be furious at me later, I thought it was cruel to ruin Avital's special weekend with such downer news. So, I kept my secret carefully buried, covering it up with an excited-to-be-having-a-girls-weekend smile. Avital deserved to be happy. Her mother had died of ovarian cancer amidst the tough first year of our general surgery internship.

Avital's sister, Nurit, had carefully scheduled the first night of our fabulously packed weekend. It had the backbreaking intensity typical of the Harari sisters. She had outlined the itinerary for us in advance via email.

-Brunch and a quick ride on the Ferris wheel at the Santa Monica pier with my chicas (exciting, check)

-Go briefly to meet the groom

-Head over to Avital's pad to shower (up-for-it, check)

-Dinner at a super cool restaurant (yummy, double check)

-Pole dancing lessons at a private studio from a slightly plump, strangely lithe 19-year-old (um, not so sure)

-Salsa dancing in the Valley (okay, I better not be sober by then)

We drove to a mind-blowing spot along the beach.

In the way of longtime friends, Avital knew something was off.

"What's going on with you? You look bothered."

"It's nothing. Just a long trip."

"I don't believe you. Tell me what's wrong."

I felt her closing in on me. Under the intensity of her glare, I caved and revealed the gut-wrenching truth. She immediately launched into huntress mode, pressing me for details.

When did I find it?

How did I find it?

What was the plan?

Why didn't I call?

I briefly responded, then tried to refocus on wedding dress designs and chuppah décor. Fortunately, we were on a tight schedule which left little time for deep conversation. A few hours later, we met up with the rest of our bachelorette posse at Avital's townhouse and began prepping for our night out. Later, at the extravagantly expensive congratulatory dinner, we micro-dined LA style and drank Merlot while pretending not to notice that B-list celebrities like Seth Rogen were sitting at adjacent tables.

By 9 pm, I found myself, in stretchy yoga pants and a tank top, in a dimly lit private studio in downtown LA. The room had several metal poles, each accompanied by a bottle of Windex and a roll of paper towels. Let me just say that I am not a very limber person. Across the room was Caroline, my coordinated polar-opposite. She was effortlessly rounding her pole for the third consecutive gyration. Caroline is good at absolutely everything. She is also my soul-sister. We first bonded in a crowded New York City bar during our surgical internship orientation. The dancing instructor glanced from her to me in disappointment as she noted my inability to engage my ankles properly for even half a turn.

Second only to my inflexibility is my inability to dance. After circling hopelessly around the freeway for an hour, by 11 pm, we arrived at a Salsa club in a seedy neighborhood somewhere in the heart of Los Angeles. Of course, Avital and her sexy six-foot tall friend Audra were prepared. They had taken several lessons in college and participated in a weekly salsa club.

After I stepped on many toes and still failed to achieve the proper rhythm, I reached the end of my rope. I glanced desperately at Avital. She was enjoying the chance to display her salsa-proficiency. By midnight, I had drained all my reserves. I had lock-jaw from faux-smiling. I turned to Essi and Caroline, who were still going strong. There was only one exit strategy and by God, I was going to take it. I shrugged, flashed a V with my fingers and simply exclaimed,

"Peace out girls, I'm playing the C-card."

I made it through the weekend in one piece. It had been a nice, helpful distraction. The strength and love of these women who had once encouraged me through the terrifying first days as a newbie surgeon-doctor now filled my diminishing reserves and emboldened me to face the frightening days ahead.

The Butterfly Effect

Sometimes I look at my children and think about how easily they could have never existed. The reason I met Alex was random and silly and shouldn't have had such a major impact on the rest of my life. But it did. I met Alex because of a picture. In general, I hate myself in all posed pictures. That summer, though, Avital took a great candid shot of me in Central Park. Somehow, she caught me looking casual-cool with that perfect sun-kissed glow. Because I now had this flattering picture, I finally caved (after months of prodding by my co-resident Vicki) and set up my JDate profile. Because I had a JDate profile, I decided at 10:30 pm on a random Saturday night to run an unfiltered search for all men of an appropriate age and height, who lived within a one-mile radius of my apartment and happened to be online at that very moment. Because Alex's handsome face popped up on my screen, I decided to IM him. We started communicating in short clever messages. Eventually, I became so tired of typing back and forth that I asked him to call me. And once I heard his kind, genuine voice, I knew that I had found the man I would marry...

This concept of one seemingly small decision causing a major downstream effect is a part of chaos theory called "the butterfly effect." This term was coined by Edward Lorenz from the metaphorical example of the details of a tornado being influenced by a minor agitation such as the distant flapping of the wings of butterflies several weeks prior. While selecting an overall method of breast reconstruction doesn't feel minor at all, the hardest part to handle is the fear of all the unknown downstream effects. For the purposes of clarity, I am going to provide a brief overview of options for breast reconstruction. Each has its own advantages and drawbacks. Depending on your plastic surgeon and his or her preference, one option may be presented more convincingly than another.

Like all areas in medicine and especially surgery, the best option is often the one the surgeon performs most frequently. That is likely to be the technique he or she has perfected over the years and therefore executes with the most finesse. That is why second and third opinions are often confusing. Most people have a hard time understanding why completely different recommendations are being presented to solve the exact same problem. As in most things, rebuilding breasts after mastectomy can be accomplished in multiple ways. You need to have a frank discussion with your surgeon to figure it out. Who do you trust to help you make that decision? How do you even understand it all without taking a class in anatomy? I wish there was an easy answer.

There are two main ways to skin the proverbial cat: using the body's own tissue (known as "flap" or autogenous reconstruction) and implant reconstruction. Flap reconstruction can sound quite Frankensteinian and scary. It boils down to this: it is based on the basic principle of blood supply. A flap is a unit of tissue that is transferred from one site (donor site) to another (recipient site) while maintaining its own blood supply. Older flap reconstruction techniques include the TRAM flap and the latissimus dorsi flap.

The TRAM flap stands for transverse rectus abdominis, a muscle in your lower abdomen between your waist and your pubic bone. A flap of this skin, fat, and all or part of the underlying rectus abdominus ("six-pack") muscle are used to reconstruct the breast. Overall, TRAM flaps are the most commonly performed type of flap reconstruction, partly because TRAM flap tissue is very similar to breast tissue and makes a good substitute. Since this technique has been around for a long time, the more senior surgeons have done them many times. The latissimus dorsi flap uses the skin, fat, and muscle (latissimus dorsi) from the back, beneath the shoulder blade area. This flap is tunneled under the skin and into the chest to create a new breast. The procedure leaves a scar on the mid-back region below the shoulder blade. The downside of TRAM and latissimus flaps is that they do cut through muscle, while other "gentler" flap reconstructions avoid this.

Newer techniques include the DIEP (deep inferior epigastric perforator flap) and other modifications. The DIEP flap is an advanced microsurgical technique in which excess living fat from bellow the belly button is transplanted to the chest to restore volume and shape. Amazingly, there are even further reconstruction techniques such as the SGAP flap (superior gluteal artery perforator) that involve transplant from other areas of unwanted excess. Although this fascinating approach was never offered to me, it might appeal to women like Beyonce or J-Lo because it results in a "butt lift" at the donor site.

Flap reconstruction is enticing to heavier women who have a large area of fat in their abdomen, inner thigh or buttocks, women who do not want to have a "foreign" material in their body and those who wish to avoid a secondary surgery. In contrast, women seeking implants for breast reconstruction are often thinner and may want to become fuller than their original breast size. When I was making my decision, multiple surgeons agreed that I didn't have enough abdominal fat to favor flap reconstruction. It was the rare time in my female adult life in which being slender limited my options.

In implant reconstruction, there are two possibilities. In one scenario, a tissue expander is inserted at the time of mastectomy. The expander is then gradually injected with saline over a period of weeks in order to stretch the tissues. In a second surgery, the expander is then exchanged for a silicone or saline implant. Alternatively, the implant can be put in place at the time of mastectomy. The implant is supported by the "implant capsule" which sounds like a cool space pod, but is, in fact, a sling or "internal bra" made up of collagen. Some surgeons prefer the two-staged approach for a fuller look because the expansion process makes room for a larger implant. In my case, this overwhelming list of menu options was omitted. Dr. Gayle made the choice simple. He offered me only one.

"You won't be happy with any flap. It won't give you enough volume or projection. Expander to implant reconstruction is the best way for you to go."

Most people won't get off this easy. Unlike me, they will need to select their reconstruction method and it's tough, no doubt. But, the reality is that you can never predict all the downstream effects of your choices. You cannot know the future. You can only gather the best available information. You rely on research and recommendations, poll your friends and family, and ask your medical friends for advice. Then, you go with your gut. After that, you cross your fingers and hope that the perturbation of your butterfly wings doesn't blow a tsunami your way.

D-Day

There is a certain sense of relief in arriving at the hospital on the day of a major surgery. The waiting part is over, and the next phase of healing begins. I was scheduled to be the first case of the day, at 7:30 am sharp. Alex and I checked in at the admissions desk of Maimonides Medical Center around 6 am. There was a very young Russian girl sitting next to us, screaming at someone on her cell phone. The hysterics of her conversation relaxed me, probably because it was impossible to think over the shrill volume of her accented voice. After about an hour of sitting and waiting, despite being the only two patients, the clerk finished processing my paperwork. Alex and I were ushered upstairs to the fourth floor.

Maimonides Medical Center's newly renovated, ultra-sleek lobby is highly deceptive. Once you exit the elevator on other floors, the interior is shabby with a striking lack of clear signage. Having mistakenly taken the wrong elevator, we exited on what we thought was our floor and were immediately lost. We began wandering in circles for at least 20 minutes, hopelessly searching for the surgical unit. Despite encountering several staff members who tried redirecting us (to other incorrect floors), a stray nurse fortuitously happened upon us and pointed us in the proper direction. Literally a few steps away, completely obstructed from our view, hung a large red sign that read "Pre-Operative Area."

Upon our arrival at the OR desk, I was shuttled into a curtained area and given two hospital gowns.

"First gown opens to the front and second to the back. Everything underneath comes off except the socks."

I can only assume this double gown policy was instituted to stop the unnecessary mooning of the hospital staff every time a patient walked down the hallway to the operating room. I stripped down as directed and sat there shivering as a litany of check-ins ensued. First, a pre-op nurse came in to ask me some screening questions. She was followed by an anesthesia resident. Later, the resident's attending re-asked the same questions regarding medications and allergies. He reiterated the risks and benefits of anesthesia. The key take-away message from all of them was that I wouldn't be awake during the surgery.

At some point, another OR nurse stopped in. Soon after her, three eager medical students popped their heads around my curtain to introduce themselves. I unceremoniously dismissed them. I know it was harsh and hypocritical. I had once been them. Still, there was no way they were going to see me completely naked and cut to pieces. Lastly, my breast surgeon, Dr. Borgen came in to review the actual details of the operation, mainly as a required formality.

Everything was going smoothly enough until it became apparent that my plastic surgeon, Dr. Gayle, was late, presumably stuck in traffic somewhere between Manhattan and Brooklyn. Soon, everyone started getting fidgety. Operating room staff

like to begin their day early in the morning. Tardiness at the
outset disrupts the entire day's schedule, so beginning the first
case on time is essential.

*"Maybe we should get started in the room. I'm sure Dr.
Gayle will be here soon."*

As a surgeon myself, I empathized with them, but I had to
stand my ground as a patient. I knew that the pre-operative
surgical marking by the attending plastic surgeon is an important ritual. It is best performed while the patient is awake and
in the upright position. I apologized while adamantly refusing
the option of being anesthetized before Dr. Gayle arrived, just
so they could get things going. Dr. Gayle ultimately did arrive
around 8 am. He was harried, with a single bead of sweat
trickling down his forehead, but he still exuded his usual calm.
He quickly did the necessary prep work, marking me up and
down, left and right. And then it was time.

My friend Rebecca Amaru, an Ob-Gyn, had sent me a video
link of a young female surgeon, Deborah Cohan, who organized
a spontaneous flash mob inside her operating room moments
before her bilateral mastectomy. The video had since gone viral
and even ended up on a Google commercial paying homage to
inspirational women. Although I appreciated her attitude and
dancing chops, I did not at all share her courage that day as I
prepared to go into the OR.

I had spent years convincing patients that there is no way
that they can wake up during anesthesia. It is a common fear
born from reports of people claiming to remember details
of their surgery or conversations amongst the surgeons and
nurses during the case. That day, I found myself terrified of
the very idea I had dismissed in others. What if I wake up and

feel the slicing through my skin? What if no one can hear my protests? Despite my fear, I plastered on a smile and got up to go empty my bladder before being brought into the operating room. Even though I had remembered to wax my bikini area for the event, I still didn't want to pee on the table before they could insert the catheter. I distinctly remember telling Alex that I would be *right back.*

When I returned from the restroom, Alex was gone from the pre-op area without a trace. I used the hospital landline to call his cell phone. He did not answer, likely because of the hospital's poor reception. My lower lip began to quiver uncontrollably. Feeling sorry for me, two nurses went searching in the hallways and waiting room. They couldn't find him. The chief resident kindly offered me his cell phone because mine was now locked away with the rest of my belongings. I texted desperately, "I didn't get to say goodbye. I love you and I'll see you soon."

All week long, I had been rehearsing this big dramatic send-off in my head:

I bravely reassure Alex that I will be fine. He professes his undying love, tears running down his face. We kiss, passionately, and they wheel me off on a stretcher...

Robbed of my moment, I felt awkward, disappointed and exposed. There was no turning back. Crushed, in my hospital issued grey sock-slippers and double-gown, I followed the surgery resident along the windy hallway into OR 1.

The only good part about being a patient in a frigid operating room, aside from the drugs, is lying down on the Bair hugger, a plastic blanket attached to a forced hot air machine, and then being covered with multiple layers of blankets straight out of the warmer. Since my patients are typically young children, I often distract them with a game of deflating and inflating the air from the Bair hugger and pretending the noises are gigantic farts. As they giggle, I hold their hands and look into their eyes while they breathe themselves to sleep. How strange to be there, lying down on the operating table, wrapped in toasty blankets. I felt the influence of the anesthetic in my veins. Dr. Gayle held my hand and looked at me with kind eyes. He uttered the words I have said a thousand times to my own patients.

"Don't worry. I will take excellent care of you."

As I began my dream of white sandy beaches and perfect blue waves, I was interrupted by the excited voice of the chief resident. He was gesticulating wildly at my feet and waving his iPhone in the air. I sleepily lifted my head to see about all the commotion.

"Wait, wait, don't fall asleep. He texted you back. He texted you back! He says, 'I love you too, Babes.'"

I lay down my head and drifted off to sleep with fearful tears running down my cheeks, but with a brave smile on my face.

Doctors Are the Worst Patients

There is absolutely nothing good to say about the first two post-operative weeks after a bilateral mastectomy and lymph node dissection. Immediately after emerging from surgery, I was severely nauseated and vomited frequently into the provided pink plastic bucket. Worse, I had been promised a private room for the entirety of my one-night hospital stay. Instead, I was assigned a crammed room with an elderly roommate whom the nurses had assured me was "a quiet old lady who wouldn't bother me one bit." Huge lie! She spent the entire night in a confused state called "sun-downing," screaming for her daughter Sandra to come rescue her from the evil men in white suits who were trying to drain her blood.

By the next morning when the nausea wore off, so did the anesthesia. I felt as if I had been hit head-on by a Mack truck and left at the side of the road to die. Every inch of my body above the waist was in pain. I needed a combination of narcotics and ibuprofen staggered every four hours just to make it tolerable. The incisional pain was the most intense, especially at the site of the lymph node dissection. I spent the week following my hospital discharge lying limply on the couch in my parents' upstairs loft, popping pain pills like tic tacs. Visitors were not allowed, including my own children. I couldn't even fake a smile.

Sleeping proved difficult and my eyes hurt too much to distract myself with television. Then, as a side effect of the round-the-clock narcotics, I developed a horrendous headache that lasted for the next three days. Since it was the strong pain medication causing the headache, I could not figure out any way to relieve it. I tried ice packs and long steamy showers to no avail. My desperate mother even hired a massage therapist to come to the house and work on my scalp and temples for hours. This alleviated the gnawing ache, temporarily. When she stopped massaging me, the pain returned in earnest. I was in a haze and my mind was dull. I should have called my surgeon for advice at this point. But, I didn't. I obstinately tried to solve my own medical problem. I didn't want to be a bother and feared being labeled as "the-whiny-patient."

In addition to my debilitating headache, my entire GI system was gradually shutting down due to something known as "narcotic bowel." Eventually, through the fog, it occurred to me that I might be inadvertently overdoing the prescription pain medications and causing some of my own problems. Don't get me wrong, I was taking my Percocet only as directed on the bottle: one to two pills every four to six hours, as needed for pain or its prevention. Clearly, though, that amount was way too much for my naive system. Overcoming my fear of unmitigated agony, I finally mustered the courage to stop all the narcotics. Within hours, my excruciating headache miraculously began to resolve. I became lucid and realized what a zombie I had been for the past week. After that, I limited myself to Motrin and Tylenol. With one key problem solved, I moved onto the next foul challenge.

I had developed severe constipation. By postoperative day four, my intestines were completely backed up. I mean, absolutely nothing was getting through those suckers, not even gas. I had spasmodic stomach pains, loss of appetite, nausea (a recurrent theme in this narrative) and malaise. Most of this may have been preventable if only I had been compliant with the stool softeners I was advised to take. But doctors make the worst patients, as I was about to prove. Although gastroenterology is not my area of expertise, I was convinced that my problem wasn't yet serious enough to warrant a trip to the ER. With the right regiment, I could still turn this mess around, gosh darn it. I just needed a plan.

Despite having several super-specialist friends easily consultable by text, I turned to my most trusted resource, the Internet. I wrote down every suggestion Google offered and sent my poor loving father off to the pharmacy with an embarrassingly long list of stool softeners, laxatives, and enemas. As a failsafe, my mother prepared for me a "digestive" tea that she had purchased in Israel at the *shuk* (market). This unsavory concoction tasted distinctly like warm castor oil. Anyway, it did not work. I proceeded to try all the over-the-counter oral remedies including Colace, Senna and Milk of Magnesia without any success. By midnight, I was desperate.

Self-administration of a fleet enema is no easy feat. I read the package instructions multiple times. Although there is only one person in the directions diagram, it is really a two-man job. Not to be too graphic (and I will be), that night, I contorted myself into positions that no one, including my husband, should ever witness. Once I completed my task, I lay on the cold tiled floor of my parents' guest bathroom and prayed to the porcelain goddess to grant me relief. For hours, I pushed and pushed and strained and writhed in pain. Finally, at exactly 3:45 am on August 18th, I gave birth to the most beautiful three-pound poopie you have ever seen. From upstairs, I texted my worried parents about my successful delivery and fell into a hard-earned slumber.

I Hate My Jackson-Pratts

The Jackson-Pratt (JP) drain is a despicable yet effective device that is implanted after surgery to drain any excess fluid that collects around the surgical bed. At the external end of each drain is a large plastic bulb that looks like a grenade. The tubing from the drain hangs very long and the proximal portion is secured in place at the skin with sutures and large, supposedly water-tight clear bandages called Tegaderms. After axillary node dissection, the Tegaderm spans the involved armpit and cannot be removed until the drains are extracted, roughly two weeks later.

During this period, you are not allowed to shave under the arm or apply deodorant. As a female obsessed with personal hygiene who traditionally applies clinical strength Secret more than once a day, these restrictions were exceptionally onerous. Within a day, I smelled like a typical NYC cab driver whenever I lifted my arm. The only way to stay fresh was to shower multiple times a day and to never break a sweat. Since I was still mostly a couch potato, the latter limitation was easily achievable. It was the frequent showering that posed the bigger problem.

Showering solo with JP drains in place is a nearly impossible task. When dressed, one can attach the drains with a safety pin to some stable article of clothing such as a bra strap or tank top. Unsecured in the shower, they dangle. As a practical solution, I was advised to use the belt from a terry cloth robe, tie it to my waist and then secure the safety pins to the belt. This complex manipulation was required early in the postoperative period when entering and exiting the shower stall was still a gargantuan challenge. Nevertheless, I repeatedly braved the water in my determination not to stink. My success level at showering was based on careful positioning and the avoidance of any bending or stretching. For the first week, I was doing rather well. Then, one day, I dropped the soap. I stared at it for nearly 10 minutes in disbelief, watching it swirl around the rim of the shower drain. For the life of me, I couldn't figure out how to retrieve it. Should I call for help?

Alex was at work and this wasn't something I wanted my mother to see. Ultimately, I cleaned my entire body with the only accessible product, Pantene conditioner. On another occasion, I forgot my cloth belt altogether. After all, I wasn't really a robe person. I stupidly stepped into the shower holding all three drains and associated tubing in my hands. Once I was sopping wet, I realized that I needed shampoo because at this point I still had hair. The only problem was that I have two hands, not four. Desperate, I tried to jerry-rig a system of attaching the drains to the shower caddy. Immediately, one of them slipped out. Soon, the bottom-heavy bulb filled with my bodily fluids was dangling in the air and yanking uncomfortably on my skin.

In addition to managing water exposure, I was instructed to empty the drains twice daily and record the outputs. Once the daily output was less than 30 cc for three consecutive days, the drains could be removed. As you may imagine, walking around with these drains under your shirt is quite cumbersome and does not make for a sexy silhouette. Normally a fan of form-fitting clothes, I had to dip back into my most amorphous maternity gear to find something appropriate to wear out of my house. Consequently, the day I was cleared for drain removal was an exciting first milestone. When I arrived at the office for this auspicious event, Dr. Gayle's nurse politely asked me if I had remembered to take an Advil or Motrin, as previously instructed. Of course, I had not.

"Never mind. Let's just get this over with."

She cut the stitches and told me to take a deep breath and hold it. She wasn't going to lie, this would be unpleasant.

"Mother of God, Ouch, I want my Mommy!!!!"

"One drain taken out, just three more to go."

I held my breath, beginning to see stars.

"Miss, are you ok? You look a bit...green."

As the nurse ran to the adjacent room to fetch me orange juice, the color drained out of my face. When I regained my composure, I found that the aftermath of drain removal is no picnic either. There was a twitchy-twangy nerve sensation at the drain sites. It was as if someone had just ripped a long plastic sheath out my chest but had forgotten that it was still attached to my insides. This, of course, was exactly what had just happened. Per the apologetic nurse, the "mild discomfort" was supposed to last for only a few seconds. In my unfortunate case, I was still feeling the reverberation 15 minutes later when I returned to my car to drive home. So, while I applaud him for his genius drain-making skills, man I freakin' hate Mr. Jackson-Pratt.

The Unscratchable Itch

In anatomy, cutaneous nerves are responsible for providing sensory innervation to the skin. There are tons of cutaneous nerves in the human body and only some of them even have names. The intercostal brachial nerve is a tiny nerve that supplies sensory input to the skin underneath your arm. It's not really a nerve you think about much. That is, not until your breast surgeon tells you that it may be permanently injured while removing the lymph nodes from your armpit. Damage to this small nerve will cause numbness of that patch of skin right where the ugly wobbly bits of your upper arm reside. When Dr. Borgen first explained it to me, it seemed like such a small sacrifice in the bigger picture of survival. I remember shrugging at his warning,

"I'm sure I won't miss it. Just don't cut any of those big nerves that move my arm and end my career!!"

I chuckled. Dr. Borgen was not amused. I immediately set aside the concern and buried it beneath so many others.

Walking back to my car, I thought about the numerous times that I counseled patients on the complications of parotidectomy, excision of the large saliva gland in the cheek. The greatest danger of parotid surgery is injury to the facial nerve (the important nerve that moves the face). That is relatively rare in benign cases. The more common complication is damage to the greater auricular nerve which provides sensation to the ear lobe and skin around the ear. Even in those cases, sensation is often regained within a year, though often a small area of skin remains forever anesthetized. When confronted with the more devastating possibility of your face being paralyzed, a little earlobe numbness doesn't sound too bad to most patients... but tell that to the unfortunate woman who is trying to put on her earrings every day.

Before breast cancer, the closest I came to dealing with this issue was some temporary numbness after dental work. Because I am petrified of the dentist, I had been loyally going to Buddy Kruger (who is now 70) for over two decades. He is the only person I've trusted in my mouth since I was a teenager. Over the years, as I moved far away from his office near my parents' home in New Jersey, getting to these appointments had become progressively more difficult. During residency, making an appointment was nearly impossible. This is probably why, by the young age of 27, I had the dental health of an 80-year-old homeless woman. When I finally did manage to squeeze in a visit, I generally needed a minimum of a root canal and two cavities drilled on the same day.

To keep me pain-free, Dr. Kruger would be forced to inject enough Novocain in my mouth to anesthetize a baby elephant. Inevitably, I would leave the office unable to feel my lips for several hours. The problem was that I was usually heading back into the City. In preparation, I always wanted to reapply my lipstick. It is a very strange thing to discover the difficulty of using use lip-liner when the skin around your mouth is numb. There is something important about that tactile feedback. You don't miss it until it's gone. Even staring straight into a mirror, I always wound up looking like a cross between Lucille Ball and a scary clown.

Now that I had surgery, the numbness that I assumed would be no big deal had become a major annoyance in my life. Aside from the injured intercostal brachial nerve, there was a second source of numbness at the mastectomy sites. This was caused by multiple small cutaneous nerves being severed from the surgical incisions. When, like me, your incision extends into the armpit, so does the area of sensory nerve injury. When a nerve is injured, the proximal (body) end of the nerve tries to heal itself. Cells called phagocytes try to clean up the mess so that the nerve cable (axon) and surrounding insulation (myelin sheath) can regenerate. The problem is that nerve regeneration in small nerves progresses at the rate of 1 mm/day. So, waiting for your cutaneous nerves to regrow is like watching paint dry...it's really, really slow. For some, the sensation is gradually regained over the course of months or weeks and for others, it never returns.

Unfortunately, unlike the Novocain, the numbness band around my incision sites has yet to wear off. This feeling of not sensing your own skin is very dissociative. It's like wearing a permanent tube top that you can't ever take off. And not only is the top permanently plastered to your skin, but also the body underneath it doesn't belong to you. I mean it's attached to you and you can see yourself pressing on it, but you may as well be touching a piece of raw meat on your cutting board.

While waiting for the numbness to resolve, you have a bigger problem to deal with: itching. The etiology of itch is not always clear and can result from many conditions such as dry skin, anxiety, stress or metabolic and endocrine disorders.

The itchiness after breast cancer surgery may be a sign of the damaged nerves regenerating. The thought that your body is trying to heal itself after such a massive insult is a nice concept to ponder. However, it doesn't make the reality any more bearable. More importantly, the problem with this kind of itching isn't just that it's uncomfortable, it is that it's unscratchable.

Unlike that irritating spot in the middle of your back that you can never reach, this is not an issue of accessibility. It cannot be relieved with a long-handled loofa brush or by teaching your children (as I have) how to give Mommy a proper back scratch. Because the skin overlying the itch is numb, you can't feel the scratch. Without feeling the scratch, you can't relieve the itch. You may think that, with the fear of painful death and dying on your hands, it would be easy to get over this. You would be wrong. The unscratchable itch can torture you every night while you lie in bed excoriating your skin with absolutely no relief.

Numbness and itching in your armpit, under your arm and across your chest is another doozy on the list of things they never tell you about breast cancer. Ask any woman who's gone through it and you'll be sure to hear,

"OMG that was THE most annoying part of it all."

Others may try to convince you that it's a small price to pay to rid yourself of cancer, and I agree. I mean, what exactly is the alternative? Still, these are the maddening details that really drive you to the brink of insanity. Thank God, for most, the itching eventually fades. The numbness may not. So, for those who know about it, better to acknowledge the problem than to downplay it. And to those poor souls who are experiencing areas of numbness firsthand, these are my only words of wisdom and comfort: just be thankful it isn't your g-spot.

I Thought I Had "The Good Cancer"

The nutty thing about my father having been recently diagnosed with an incurable type of cancer was that everyone kept referring to me as having "the good cancer." Friends of the family used this catchphrase to reassure my mother that things weren't as bad as they seemed.

"At least you don't have to worry about Tali too much. Her cancer is easily treatable."

Other things also detracted from my due sympathy. Our family and friends were amazed at my father's hasty recovery from brain surgery. Mine, in contrast, was perceived as oddly sluggish. I was hurt by this widespread minimization of my life-threatening situation. What most people don't know is that the surgery to remove a brain tumor is, surprisingly, quite painless because there are no sensory nerves in the brain. On the other hand, the chest muscles and skin overlying the breasts are exquisitely sensitive. Also, there is no cosmetic deformity left after the removal of cancerous brain tissue except for a gigantic scar across the scalp. I was left physically disfigured. Still, I couldn't argue with the notion that, at the very least, my breast cancer was curable. No need to worry about dying or anything serious like that. I should be around for several more decades, plenty of time to raise my young family. Or so I thought...

My absolute rock bottom was the day I received my surgical pathology results. Again, I made the mistake of taking the doctor-shortcut. My breast surgeon, Dr. Borgen, was on vacation for the two weeks immediately following my mastectomy. As an informed and impatient surgeon, I knew pathology results only took a week to be finalized. Expecting no surprises, I begged Natalie to get the results in advance of Borgen's return. This was a mistake. I promised her I'd act appropriately surprised at my follow-up appointment which was scheduled for the following Tuesday. She hesitated. Under duress, she complied. She texted me a picture of the three-paged results. Reading it in concert, we were both faced with shockingly grave news. Here are the highlights:

"18 out of 24 lymph nodes positive for cancer." "Evidence of lymphovascular invasion." "Diffuse micrometastasis."

All very bad features! What happened to the tumor that I had supposedly caught early? What about the single rogue lymph node that had been completely excised?

I think it's worth taking a moment to clarify breast cancer staging. There is actually a Stage 0, which is also called "non-invasive" or carcinoma in situ. This is when the abnormal cancer cells have not spread outside the ducts or the lobules into surrounding breast tissue. Starting from Stage 1, the breast cancer is called invasive, meaning it has broken free to attack healthy tissue. From there, it progresses to Stages 2, 3 and 4. Stage 3 cancer means that the breast cancer has extended beyond the immediate region of the tumor to other nearby areas such as the lymph nodes and muscles. It has not yet spread to distant organs. Although this stage is considered to be advanced or "locally metastatic," there are still treatment options that are known to be effective and the cancer is still considered curable.

Stage 3 breast cancer is subdivided into three groups: Stage 3A, 3B, and 3C. The difference is determined by the size of the tumor and how much surrounding tissue and lymph nodes contain cancer. In short, the higher the number and letter, the more extensive the disease and the higher the chance of recurrence. My stage was advanced because of the number of my axillary lymph nodes that contained cancer rather than the size of the original tumor. In metastatic breast cancer, or Stage 4, the cancer has spread beyond the breast to distant sites such as the lungs, bone, distant lymph nodes, liver or brain. At that point, the cancer is no longer curable, although it can be controlled with medications. People can live for a long while with their disease contained, but they will never be "cancer-free."

Based on my quick assessment from another feverish Google search, all these tumor-filled lymph nodes landed me at Stage 3C, the worst category out of choices A, B or C. This was a terrible, though not the worst, place to be given that cancer has only four stages. It changed the game. Pre-operatively, Borgen had promised me only a 50-50 chance of requiring chemo and no possibility of needing radiation. Suddenly, the treatment course stretched out before me like an interminably long road. Fourteen weeks of chemotherapy was now a definite, followed by five to six weeks of exhausting radiation. When would I be able to return to work? More importantly, could this disease kill me?

I cried myself to sleep each night imagining my daughters

growing up motherless. According to the National Institute of Cancer's website, my chance for a complete cure had just plummeted from the mid-90s to somewhere in the 40 percent range. When I met my friend Rachel, a well-respected cognitive behavioral psychologist (who *should* have known better), for dinner, I was still reeling from the news.

"Wait, if you have a 49 percent chance of disease-free survival, that means you have a 51 percent chance of dying!"

*"**YES**. Thanks for the math lesson."*

This came from a woman who is professionally trained to alter people's negative perceptions and to treat anxiety and depression. Shit, I'm screwed!

As it turns out, Dr. Borgen had a convenient theory that placed me back around the 90% cure rate. It took another week for me to hear his optimistic view, during which time I drew up my will. I had researched will documentation several years prior, right after Scarlett was born. I had even printed out several templates and convinced Alex to meet me at Barnes and Noble, a quiet and neutral place, to discuss it. I thought we might argue over to whom we would leave our children in the unlikely event that we both died. Alex was reluctant to discuss the subject of dying. He thought that I was being morbid. Although we reached a verbal agreement, we never completed any documents. What was the likelihood we would both die young anyway? Now only four years later, reading my pathology results, I was face to face with my mortality.

Dr. Borgen's interpretation was worth the wait. He explained that my tumor was relatively innocent, as malignant tumors go. Yet, just by chance, it happened to be growing near a large lymphatic channel.

"Think of it as a not particularly aggressive driver who suddenly finds himself on the Audobahn. The average tumor should only be able to drive at a rate of 60 mph. Your tumor just happened to jump on the superhighway going 100 mph. As a result, it was able to spread quickly, spraying little tumor seeds everywhere in the axillary node system."

Great, just my luck. And I don't even speed.

The point of Borgen's analogy was that he believed my cancer was still highly curable. It was just going to take a lot more time and effort to get there. In future appointments, my medical oncologist would independently come up with a similar perspective. With both of my oncologic doctors supporting this theory, I decided to buy into the whole positive interpretation of my lousy pathology results. At that point, I had nothing to lose.

Managing Regret

Once it was clear that the "thank-God-you-caught-it-early tumor" was, in fact, advanced, the burning question of how long it had been there ping-ponged relentlessly in my brain. More to the point, could it have been detected earlier? I think it's natural for people who are given a devastating diagnosis to mull over the past, searching for clues, mistakes that, if corrected, may have yielded a different outcome. Like Cher, we often wish we could find a way to turn back time.

There was one comment made by my Ob-Gyn that really brought this issue to the forefront. I came in to see him after my biopsy proved that I had an estrogen/progesterone responsive tumor. The purpose of the visit was to replace my IUD. A few months prior, at my six-week post-partum visit, he had implanted a Mirena Intrauterine Device (IUD) as a birth control measure. This IUD releases synthetic progestin hormone to prevent the ovaries from releasing an egg. Now, my oncologist didn't like the idea of having extra progesterone hormones circulating in my system, even if it was just locally in my cervix. Although the scientific literature was not clear on this issue, no one on my medical team wanted to take a risk. So, while I was in his office getting my Mirena switched out for the traditional copper IUD, he casually mentioned,

"I can't be sure. My guess is that you probably already had cancer during your pregnancy and that was why you developed preeclampsia. As I said before, preeclampsia is so rare in a third pregnancy with the same father. It was like your body was starting to go haywire and signaled that your baby needed to come out... of course, there was nothing unusual on your breast exam during your pregnancy, because I checked my computerized notes and I wrote 'no findings'."

This theory that the cancer had already been present during my pregnancy with Milla made sense because these hormone-sensitive breast tumors are typically slow growing. By the same token, my tumor was almost definitely palpable several months prior to my discovering it, because, by then, it was already pretty large. So, this begged the question, "did my doctors miss something?"

As a surgeon, I see many patients for second opinions. I also see many disgruntled patients who are unhappy with the care they previously received because they feel something important was overlooked. I always counsel them the same way.

"We can't go back in time. We need to fix the problem, and not waste our energy trying to figure out what might have been if someone had intervened earlier. Most likely, it wouldn't have changed the outcome."

The reason for my repeated assertion is not just a physician's creed to "protect our own." Our first loyalty is always to the patient. It's that this line of thinking is counterproductive. Patients or parents of patients are already pissed off. I find that defusing their anger, even when it is justified, and helping them to move forward is a much better approach than allowing them to dwell on the past.

What about me? Could I apply this same logic to my own situation? It's tough because it was a definitive time, rare in fact because I was under the consistent care of another doctor. During this unique period, I trusted that I was being properly monitored, especially in the girlie parts arena. I'd like to let it go. I want to believe that even if I had, in fact, already had cancer during that time that it could not have been detectable. Because if I accept that truth, then I can't be mad at myself or anyone else for failing me. I wish it was that simple. But there was this thought that kept banging at the door of my memory, demanding to be let in. Then one sleepless night, about two months after my diagnosis, when the chaos of the devastating news died down and all its implications had sunk in, the door suddenly opened... I had felt a lump before!

After Milla was born prematurely, her digestive system was way too immature to process food so, she was fed intravenously. Even once she was able to tolerate breast milk, she was too weak to feed directly from the breast. Immediately after her birth, the NICU team encouraged me to stockpile breast milk for her. Consequently, when I came to the hospital to visit my tiny pumpkin, I would hook up to this powerful hospital-issued breast pump. Most of the time, I pumped behind a portable divider erected around her isolet. Sometimes, to give me more privacy, the nurses let me sit alone in a small room with a rocking chair adjacent to the NICU. One day, while I was fitting myself into the milking apparatus, I felt a mass in the corner of my left breast.

"That's weird," I remember thinking. I wasn't concerned

because it was small and mobile. I did call over one of the more seasoned nurses,

"Can you take a feel of this? What do you think it is?"

"Feels like a blocked milk duct. It's common. You should just massage it daily while you're pumping to try to work it out."

"Ok, thanks."

And so, I did just that.

I would have dismissed the whole thing out of my mind completely. Except, a few days later, I was sitting and chatting with my friend Sophia in the backrow benches of our synagogue after services. Sophia's daughter, Emma, had been born full term in perfect health, in the same week and at the same hospital as my Milla. Sophia was telling me that she was on antibiotics for mastitis, an infection of the breast tissue that occurs most frequently during breast feeding. It is often secondary to a blocked milk duct. I recall our conversation clearly because she was complaining that it was super annoying and hurt like hell. I remember thinking that I was so lucky because my blocked duct hadn't become infected and didn't bother me at all. I poked at it a few more times over the following weeks. It was about one centimeter in diameter, about the size of a penny. After that, I just forgot completely about my presumably benign lump that wasn't causing any problems anyway...

To this day, I cannot swear that the lump I felt was on the left, more specifically in the upper outer quadrant where my tumor was later located. However, it's suspicious. Right? Four months later, I find a honkin' cancerous breast mass. What are the odds? I told very few friends about this. I was embarrassed because it put the onus of earlier discovery onto me. Those friends that I did tell blew it off anyway because lumpy breasts are common during pregnancy and rarely signify anything ominous. My Ob-Gyn was adamant that he had felt nothing unusual on my physical exam. I'd like to give him the benefit of the doubt. But this nagging, gnawing feeling of regret was tenacious. It forced me to ask questions that I couldn't answer:

What if I had gone directly to my doctor and made him feel the lump?

Would he have imaged it?

Even if that particular lump was benign, wouldn't he have found the real cancer?

What would have happened if I had caught it that much earlier?

Would I still have needed chemotherapy? Radiation? A decade of Tamoxifen?

Would my chances of survival have been much higher?

Would my risk of recurrence have been drastically lower?

These burning questions tunneled deep into the furrows of my brain. I found myself struggling to let go of the same sentiments I discouraged in my patients and their families.

This brings me to the subject of breast cancer screening and my shameless plug not to ignore it. Breast cancer screening wouldn't have helped me. I had no family history. I had no known genetic risk and I was less than 40 at the time of my diagnosis. So, why am I pushing for it now? Well, the goal of screening tests for breast cancer is to find it before it causes symptoms like a lump that can be felt. The advantage of early detection is identifying disease when it is more easily treatable and, if you are lucky, still confined to the breast. The other advantage is a psychological one. About 1 in 8 U.S. women (about

12%) will develop invasive breast cancer over the course of her lifetime.[1] That's a lot. Knowing you did everything in your power not to be a part of that statistic is a powerful thing.

Amongst various agencies, there is an ongoing debate regarding when to begin breast cancer screening. Currently, the American Cancer Society, the American College of Radiology and the Center for Disease Control do not unanimously agree. In October 2015, the American Cancer Society (ACS) released their new guidelines for women at average risk for breast cancer.[2] Among the changes, the new recommendations stated that all women should begin having yearly mammograms at age 45 and can switch to every other year beginning at age 55. The rules for younger women (ages 40 to 44) are vague, suggesting these women should be able to start the screening as early as age 40 if they want to. For those at high risk due to definable factors such as genetics, family history or previous exposure to radiation, it is a different story. The recommendations for that subpopulation, which will apply to my daughters, are more stringent.

A surprising change in the newer guidelines is that breast exams, either from a medical provider or self-exams, are no longer recommended. Apparently, research has not shown a statistical benefit. The ACS does add, "women should be familiar with how their breasts normally look and feel and report any changes to a healthcare provider right away." [3]

Ok, thanks, man. What does that mean?

My only advice is to poke around in there. See what the terrain is like and don't be shy. True, it may lead to some scares and false alarms. Speak up nonetheless. Think of me as your cautionary tale. Finding a lump on your own terms may not change your prognosis, but you'll kick yourself if someone else finds it later. Also, don't be silly and ignore anything you do find. Avoidance is never the right move, especially when it comes to cancer. Remorse will taunt you. Then, like me, you'll spend your life wondering if things could have been different... only, if only...you could turn back time.

The Pity Face

With the unexpected turns my life had taken, I experienced numerous gestures of friendship. Despite the benefit of this new-found popularity, there is a downside to becoming the object of everyone's sympathetic attention. Whenever you speak, people inadvertently give you what I call "the sad, sad face." I double the sad because, in my case, there was double the cancer given my father's malignancy. That meant I got a second dose of sympathy even though the first was already too much. To make this characteristic face, one must furrow the brow deeply and purse the top lip as if beginning to cry. It is an easily recognizable and highly reproducible expression. In person, I do a great imitation. Because this is a book, you'll just have to imagine it for yourself.

I observed my first example of this worried countenance on the face of our community Rabbi. Alex and I live a Modern Orthodox lifestyle. This means that we keep a kosher home and observe the laws of Sabbath. Otherwise, we are fully integrated into mainstream society and often "cheat" on the details. We are involved in communal life. We attend synagogue on all Jewish holidays, of which there are many, and most Saturdays unless the weather is threatening, or we are lazy. We chose

White Plains as a place to live because of its open-minded, family-oriented and intelligent Jewish community.

The night we received my pathology results, my deeply upset husband had summoned Rabbi Marder to our home to discuss the whole "why do bad things happen to good people" existential dilemma. We all sat down at our dining room table, drank tea with chocolate wafers and searched for answers to unanswerable questions.

"Why us? Why now? Why both my father and me?"

As Alex unloaded the burdensome details of my predicament, I noted the characteristic head tilt, sympathetic nod, and troubled eyes. Soon, my heart started pounding, my blood pressure began rising, and I became unusually hot. I felt trapped under the magnifying glass of compassion. After several intense minutes of silence, the Rabbi's face finally relaxed, and our conversation drifted back into the mundane.

"How is the baby sleeping?"

"Are you in need of any household supplies?"

He mentioned that his son's wet cough had finally resolved. The constant congestion remained.

"Should we continue with the nasal steroid spray?"

Reverting to my familiar role as the neighborhood ENT was just what I needed to defuse my mounting tension.

"Yes. I'll call in a refill."

Truth be told, I could hardly represent a more unfortunate character, so I get it.

Young doctor-mom with two toddlers and a new baby who was recently discharged after a prolonged stay in the Neonatal Intensive Care Unit (NICU) now diagnosed with Stage 3 breast cancer, plus a father with glioblastoma...

It was a story that could redden even the most hardened stranger's eyes. Maybe if I also had a dog with one leg, a recent house fire or was caring for a sick, elderly grandmother, I could drum up a tad more sympathy, but not much.

Most of the time I vacillated widely between my disdain for pity and the recognition that I had been dealt a raw deal. I should have understood how hard it was for the people around me to toe the proper line. It reminds me of the weekend I told my friend Karen. I pulled her into the living room and sat her down on the couch in a very serious manner.

"I have some bad news," I said with a downcast gaze, pausing for effect.

"I have **cancer.***"*

"What kind?"

"Breast."

"Oh, that's it. Phew, you scared me. I thought it was something worse. That's easy, you can kick that."

Wait, what the...?

Karen's response was the other extreme, way too nonchalant, not sympathetic enough. It wasn't until days later that she apologized for the flippancy of her reaction. She and her husband Seth are close friends of ours. Their daughter Jordana is my daughter Juliette's best friend. I know Karen cares deeply about me. She thought positivity was the best response. In her mind, she had immediately decided that I would get better. Because I *had* to because our daughters *had* to grow up together and we all *had* to be there as parents raising them together. Wasting time on tears just wasn't her thing.

Throughout my ordeal, Karen's optimistic attitude really came in handy. Later, in the throes of chemo, I would walk to her house whenever I wanted to be treated completely normally. Our combined six kids would play while the grown-ups drank wine and snacked on chips and salsa. Alex and Seth would eventually wander to the garage to attack the giant punching bag and Karen and I would hang back in the kitchen. She would always start off by asking me how I was doing, then easily shift over to a discussion about her job and the legal cases she was working on. No one in the house seemed to dwell on my lack of hair or my gauntness. No one rushed to tie my children's shoes or to change Milla's stinky diapers.

Fortunately, there were some other couples who were also comfortable treating me normally, Malka and Stevie, Lisa and David, Dena and Jon and Ari and Lauren, to name a few... In their homes, I was the same old high-functioning Tali. In the outside world, it was nice to know that people worried about me. Overall, it was good to have that balance. Too many people in my pity party and I might start believing that's where I belonged.

FALL

When Friends Come Out
of the Woodwork

You must understand how Memorial Sloan Kettering Cancer Center (MSKCC) functions to appreciate how lucky I was to see Dr. Shari Goldfarb within days of receiving my pathology results. She is a top breast oncologist in her field. One must typically jump through several hoops just to get an appointment. MSKCC is a well-oiled machine with many administrative layers and checkpoints. If any of your pre-visit testing was done elsewhere, they require a myriad of radiology reports, operative notes and pathology slides. These items must be submitted for review before you are permitted to schedule an appointment.

Even once an appointment is granted, there is typically a three-to-four week wait to see the doctor for any non-emergency situation. Despite the rules, I slipped in that morning thanks to Miki. I sat down in the cushy chair opposite Dr. Goldfarb, mesmerized by her four-carat engagement ring and long blond hair. Faced with a slew of radiology disks jammed into my purse, some crumpled, photocopied operative and pathology reports and *absolutely* no slides, Dr. Goldfarb was still wonderful to me and Alex. She patiently made lists and drew diagrams that really helped Alex process the overwhelming information, much of which he was seeing for the first time.

To her further credit, Miki pursued me throughout my course of treatment with the tenacity of a stalker, despite my tendency to screen and ignore phone calls when I was feeling down. Like Natalie, she relieved me of much of the burden of figuring out what to do and how to get the best care. We talked about the options and reached conclusions together using the terms and shorthand that we learned during our four years together in medical school. Because of their combined efforts, I was never alone in making critical decisions for myself. I trust I never will be.

As undeniably fortunate as I have been to have medically connected and knowledgeable friends in my corner, I was surprised to discover how restorative my "unconnected friends" could be.

One of the positive byproducts of shuttling during the day between my own doctor's appointments and that of my father was my frequent ability to call my oldest and dearest friend Avigail. Avigail is a stunningly beautiful, brilliant half-Iraqi half-Moroccan Israeli who I met in seventh grade. In the small town of Allentown, Pennsylvania where I grew up, her auspicious arrival during middle school was one of the turning points in my life. Her parents were both teachers who came on loan from Israel for a few years to teach Hebrew language at my school. From the moment we first met, Avigail and I were like peas in a pod. We studied, spent weekends together, commuted and bonded constantly right up until mid-high school when her family moved back home. We had one near feud over a lame dude named David. That was about it.

For the three years after she moved away, we spent summers alternating between our respective countries of residence, working jobs together and living in each other's homes. Texting and email were non-existent in the early days after our separation in sophomore year of high school. We were relegated to writing each other letters using what millenials call "snail mail." In recent years, she had taken a job which involved a substantial amount of travel internationally, including to the United States. The strength of our friendship, which had spanned decades, was nourished during those brief, in-person rendezvous in New York City.

Now, finally, for the first time in 15 years, the seven-hour-ahead time difference in Jerusalem worked in my favor. While I was driving to morning appointments, Avigail was often commuting home from work. When I was waiting impatiently to talk to my father's radiation oncologist, Avigail and I could connect. One time, I sat for an hour in my parked car outside of Hackensack Hospital in New Jersey just to finish our chat. She understood me empirically and she knew my father well. She grasped my attachment and the agony of possibly losing him. I felt less alone, less scared knowing I could call her and hear her non-drowsy reassuring voice at any time.

Another person who reemerged from my past was my best friend and roommate from college, Miriam Shaviv, who as a young adult had also moved to Israel. When Miriam found out about my situation, she booked a ticket to JFK for the week after my surgery. I tried to tell her not to come. But, in my heart, I was overjoyed. No matter how great new friends can become, old friends are more like family. You can burden them with your sadness and pain without feeling you need to entertain them with sarcasm and jokes. Miriam is insanely intuitive, funny and warm and she perceived me in a way that no one else did. She accepted my quirky insecurities and deep-seated body image issues, already present at the time we met during freshman orientation at age 18. She had always been my biggest fan and the first to postulate that my failure with men in college was due to their intimidation by my intelligence and beauty, rather than my shortcomings. Hey, you gotta love that theory.

By the time Miriam arrived, I was starting to unravel. Milla was not been sleeping at all. Additionally, she was battling a diaper rash so severe that the skin all over her tiny tooshie and "bagina," as her sister Scarlett called it, was completely raw. I still had limited left shoulder mobility. My older girls were adjusting poorly to my recent prolonged absence while recuperating at my parents' home. They were clinging to me like barnacles. Everyone in the house was constantly crying, including me. In short, my world was in upheaval and I was on the brink of a meltdown. Miriam swooped in, jet-lagged but determined to make it better.

For the entire week she was with us, Miriam chauffeured me around to my various appointments. Once, to secure the most coveted parking spot outside of Dr. Gayle's Brooklyn office, she waited for me in the driveway for an entire hour. When I finally returned to the car despondent, she made me laugh hysterically at several well-crafted yet inappropriate Chassidic jokes. As I soaked in her presence, she spent her time on alert for other areas in my life that required attention and grew concerned for Alex as well. Miriam recognized the torment behind his smile, the exhaustion behind his graciousness. She sensed that he was desperate to unload. On her last night, though she was leaving on a red-eye flight the next morning, she asked him out for a drink under the pretense that she needed to get out of our house. I knew she was wiped, having spent the entire visit sleeping on the floor of Milla's room on a lumpy blow-up mattress. Compounding that, she was returning home to manage her own three young kids' hectic schedules. Tired and still recovering, I fell asleep on the couch as soon as they left. I don't know what they talked about. They were gone for many hours. What I do know is that the next morning, Alex had the easy smile of a man unburdened. Only Miriam could have done that for me.

While Miriam was in town, she galvanized three of my other powerhouse friends to visit me: Aviva, Shlomit, and Tamar. Aviva was a super smart plastic surgeon in Manhattan with twin toddlers and a baby at home. She ran a wildly successful boutique practice on the Upper East Side of Manhattan to earn money and covered trauma surgery at Harlem Hospital to keep her skills sharp and give back to society. She was also my roommate in medical school and married to my former ENT chief resident. Aviva was a skilled perfectionist and I trusted her opinion completely. Beyond that, she trained under Dr. Gayle during fellowship. Her faith in his skills was one of the main reasons that I chose him as my plastic surgeon. Like Natalie, she was one of the first people I called for advice while initially panicking. Although we hadn't been in regular touch, she quickly involved herself in the details of my care. We both agreed that it would be better for her to help me identify the right surgeon rather than be that surgeon herself. There are times when things just hit too close to home.

Shlomit was a busy musculoskeletal radiologist in New Jersey, also insanely intelligent and capable. She had four very young kids. We had been friends since sleep away camp and had studied obsessively for our MCATs (Medical College Admission Test) together.

Tamar was a giving, devoted mother and sharp lawyer who lived in New Rochelle with three kids including a six-month-old infant.

Bringing this crew together was an impressive feat. Surrounded by three old friends, I felt like myself again. Post-surgery, it was the first time I dressed in ordinary fitted clothing. The four of them toasted me for venturing out in public so soon. I was blown away by their eagerness to gather on my account. By the time Miriam left, she had tasked each of these hardworking individuals with the additional job of keeping a close eye on me and providing her with updates via WhatsApp and Facebook.

Tamar took the responsibility seriously. She started texting and emailing me daily from the moment Miriam flew back to Israel. At this point, I was still unable to drive. She offered to do errands and by that Sabbath weekend, a huge food delivery arrived from the local Kosher take-out restaurant replete with a main dish, four sides, grape juice and two challahs. Inspired by Miriam's visit, Tamar decided that improving my convalescence was her new personal mission. Her persistence despite little encouragement from me, was amazing. She made countless offers to meet me for breakfast or lunch, or to pick me up for coffee after dropping off her kids and before starting her workday. At some point, I casually mentioned that I needed a new bathmat for our main bathroom. My girls had been slipping in the bathtub and peppering their little knees with black and blue marks. The next day, Tamar ran to Bed Bath and Beyond, purchased a fancy bamboo mat, dropped the bag at my doorstep and then refused to let me pay her for it.

Do you know those friends in life that you always liked and wished you were closer with? That's what Tamar was like for me and I tried to take this unfortunate opportunity in my life to renew and strengthen my relationships. Sometimes, though, even people like Tamar can be too nice. Let me give you a perfect illustration.

In an attempt to save money, Alex had been doing all the yard work. He purchased a lawnmower and a weed whacker and was spending several hours on Sunday afternoons trimming the hedges and ripping out perfectly good shrubbery. He then gathered all the grass clippings and branches and dumped them on the front lawn right near the driveway with every intention of cleaning them up. Like many men, he never finished the job. As a result, piles of sharp branches and other debris were sticking out dangerously in all directions, some of them lying perpendicular to the tires of the three cars we parked tightly along our narrow driveway.

Tamar came to pick me up for coffee soon after Alex had promised for the third time to clean up his mess *today*. She immediately noticed the unruly piles of foliage debris. So, after she dropped me back at the house, she drove twenty-five minutes to The Home Depot in New Rochelle. There she bought two boxes of large Hefty contractor black bags and returned to my house to collect the branches herself. Ok, I know I had cancer and it was lousy... But, instead of cleaning up our mess, she should have insisted we hire a damn gardener.

Insomnia and Netflix

I thank God for my friends. I am equally grateful to the Lord for Reed Hastings, co-founder of Netflix. During the first six post-surgical weeks, I was under strict orders to sleep in the supine position. The reason for this unusual form of torture is to avoid putting undue pressure on the newly inserted faux-boob tissue expanders. Since I spent my entire childhood and adulthood sleeping curled on my side or belly, laying on my back was incompatible with sleep. I found myself wide awake, night after night, listening to the changing breathing patterns of my snorting, snoring husband. My worried mother urged me to take an Ambien or just half a Lunesta. She was convinced that proper rest was the cure for all my ailments. In retrospect, I should have listened. I didn't. Instead, I was stubborn, concerned that if I started taking sleeping pills, I'd never fall asleep again without them.

In my non-cancerous real life, I was responsible for being alert through the wee hours of the night. Not just as a mother, preparing bottles and clumsily changing diapers in the glow of the nightlight, but as a physician, taking patient phone calls and making decisions that affected peoples' health. For ten days each month, I was on call 24 hours a day for a major medical center, a community hospital, the transfer center for several smaller nearby hospitals, and all the patients in my practice. I was also on unofficial backup for pediatric airway emergencies that my on-call colleagues were not as comfortable handling. With lives at stake, there was never an excuse for sleeping through a hospital page. Although during this time I was completely off-duty, I was afraid of developing a dependency on those magical little pills that promised the gift of slumber. So, sick of counting sheep and drinking gallons of warm milk, I accepted insomnia as my "frenemy" and turned for comfort to my most steady lover, the television.

Totally set-up with the Roku controller, I began voraciously devouring anything on Netflix with multiple seasons, attractive actors and mindless plots. During my early recovery period, I plowed my way through three seasons of USA's *White Collar* until I found out that the super-hot main character was gay, thus fizzling my interest due to the impossibility of our eventual union. *Nurse Jackie* hit the spot because Eddie Falco is an awesome actress and there are 7 seasons of the show. Also, I love watching medical personnel with major character flaws because let's face it, we're all human. For a while, I got more serious. I started BBC's, *Downton Abbey*. After Season 1, I decided to quit when a friend accidentally revealed that Lady Sybil died of eclampsia at the end of Season 2. This storyline hit too close to home, given my recent experience with Milla's birth. Desperate for levity with more charming British accents, I turned to *The Mistresses*. This miniseries teased me with its complicated love entanglements, then ended abruptly after only one season.

Someone recommended *The Americans*, a spy drama set

during the Cold War of the Regan era. I was a fan of Kerri Russell from her "Felicity" days. Although it was irritating that Kerri was pretty, skinny and hadn't aged a bit, I wasn't jealous because she still had tiny little girl boobs. The main male character, Phillip, reminded me of my husband, who had also grown up in the former-USSR. He was strong, handsome and looked dashing in a suit. The show was well-written, perfectly cast and it was fun to remember how badly we all dressed in the 80s. Still, I had to stop watching midway through the first season. I became too paranoid and began believing, which I had already suspected, that Alex was also a sleeper agent.

My father suggested *House of Cards* which had several seasons and lots of promise. I quickly became consumed by the diabolical plot line. More importantly, Robin Wright Penn had the perfect haircut. I knew it was the look I wanted after my hair fell out from chemo and grew back again. It was smart and sleek with carefully-spaced blond low-lights, flattering from every angle. I had never worn bangs before. Shaped the right way, I was convinced I could pull them off. I saved a picture to my iPhone and walked around with it like Robin was my friend. One day in the future, I would show it to my hairdresser and say,

"This is exactly the style I want."

Back at home, I continued my all-night channel surfing. Alex was kind to me. He lied and told me that the glow and hum of the TV did not interrupt his sleep. Though he tossed and turned and covered his head with a pillow, he rarely asked me to shut it off. In return, I often flipped on the closed captioning and listened at volumes compatible only with lip-reading. Much to my frustration, every night between the hours of 1 and

5 am, I lay in bed, awake and exhausted. I was zombie-like, staring at the screen until my eyes were numb. It was a very lonely existence, interrupted only by the multiple awakenings of my children: Milla around 11 pm and 4 am for a bottle, Juliette around five am for pee-pee, then finally the Scarlett-Juliette combo at 6 am for good.

Luckily, in addition to Netflix, we had FIOS, which included premium channels and on-demand television. Eventually, I re-watched every iconic movie from the 90s. Tom Cruise was especially good to me when his *Top Gun, Days of Thunder* and *Far and Away* trifecta helped me through a miserable night. I promised myself that I wouldn't watch *The Big C*, a series on Showtime in which Laura Linney plays a woman diagnosed with incurable metastatic melanoma. After all, I was using television for an escape, not an extra dose of reality. Then, I caved, with mixed results. At first, I was really pissed at the main character's selfishness. She used cancer as her justification for sleeping around and ignoring her husband and kid. Over time, I warmed to her. Who am I to say what it feels like to be given a zero percent chance of surviving the year? It can't feel good.

I tried to balance serious drama with comic levity. Did I mention that Julia Louis-Dreyfuss absolutely kills it on the HBO series, *VEEP*? The quick-witted biting Washington sarcasm in that show slays me. Those HBO writers always screw you in the end. They addict you for a few seasons and then inevitably abandon you for a three-year hiatus. Preparing myself, I carefully treated each episode like a bar of Toblerone... small bites, Tali...small bites. Despite my best attempts, I eventually caught up to the most current shows. Once again becoming desperate, I revisited my favorite episodes. Then, I begrudgingly started watching *Homeland*, a series I had been purposely avoiding because I found Claire Dane's emotional instability as a CIA operative rather annoying. I mean, I know, you're bipolar and constantly thwarting terrorist plots against the United States, but get it together girl, things could be worse... trust me.

Parking Wars

Once I recovered from surgery enough to solidify my next move, it was already late to be choosing an oncologist. Luckily, I had already met Dr. Goldfarb. She was fantastic, although young and my contemporary. It scared me that she didn't have the decades of seasoned experience that I associated with wiser decision making. On the other hand, I realized that this problem of mine wasn't going away anytime soon. A young doctor who could stick with me over the next several decades (if I made it that far) was better than a gray-haired, soon-to-retire physician. Either way, I found this selection process daunting. I was designating my guardian against cancer, and I had better get it right. Naturally, everyone around me had a strong opinion about who was *the absolute best*.

My friend Yonina's mother-in-law, Gail, is a well-connected woman in the New York society scene. She is also a breast cancer survivor and advocate. Luckily, she continues to do well even after a serious recurrence many years back. Gail expressly referred me to Dr. Norton, the Physician-in-Chief for breast cancer programs at Memorial Sloan Kettering. She even phoned ahead to his secretary on my behalf. I thought I had my "in".

When I called the following day, name dropping had little to no effect on the woman at the other end of the line. I was offered a consultation date in six weeks. My voice started to shake as I explained how I was expressly advised to start chemotherapy treatment within three to four weeks of my mastectomy. Two weeks had already passed, and the clock was ticking. I angled myself for sympathy, dropping words like "advanced cancer," "widespread to the lymph nodes," "e-m-e-r-g-e-n-c-y." She didn't budge. As a final ditch effort, I played the doctor card. I described the four long months I had toiled away in the Memorial operating rooms under the tutelage of their respected head and neck surgeons. That tactic also failed. Norton's schedule was harder to penetrate than Fort Knox and those days, I was running low on aggressive energy. Even if I had succeeded, I wasn't sure it was worth dragging myself into New York City every two weeks for chemotherapy.

Despite my reservations, the appeal of the Goliath-like institution lured me in. Still, I was unable to meet with Dr. Norton in time. I scheduled my first round of chemo at the Memorial Sloan Kettering building located on 66th between First and Second Avenue, under the care of Dr. Goldfarb. It was a mere three blocks away from Cornell Medical School, where a decade ago, I had been molded into a doctor.

The Evelyn H. Lauder Breast Cancer Center is a beautiful building which opened in September 2009. It is designed like a fancy hotel with sleek architecture, an impressive lobby and tufted couches in the elevators. Each floor has a grand waiting room with free snacks and flavored coffee dispensed by complex coffee-cappuccino machines. Your choice of beverage can be enjoyed on comfortable leather loveseats arranged in a circle around an intricate administrative area. All the bathrooms are super clean and highly automated with marble countertops. It wasn't a warm environment, but its established reputation as a mecca of oncologic treatment made me feel safe. These docs were the big boys of cancer. They must know how to put up a good fight, right?

My mother joined me for my first infusion of Adriamycin and Cytoxan. The experience was mostly uneventful, aside from the irritating burning sensation in my nose and overall awfulness of being pumped full of caustic drugs.

The more traumatic event occurred when we retrieved our car. We had parked in the designated garage across the street which was expensive, but convenient. In the morning when we arrived, we mistakenly assumed that we would get a significant patient discount. We were incorrect.

By the time we emerged from the building, it was already evening. My mom and I returned to the garage physically spent and emotionally drained. We handed in our ticket. The fee was a steep $60 even after the measly 10% discount offered to patients. This annoyed my mother, who is used to friendly New Jersey hospitals with their spacious, free parking lots. Exhausted, she said nothing and begrudgingly paid the attendant. We headed towards our car which had been pulled in front of the garage office. A few steps later, I realized that I had lost my wallet.

The problem was that I had no idea where to look. I barely remembered all the places I'd been and certainly not the sequence in which I'd visited them. I had made many stops on my Memorial journey: the registration desk, the phlebotomy lab, the first waiting room, the exam room, the second waiting room, the chemo suite, and multiple bathrooms. I was worn out and weary. I couldn't imagine walking back up the ramp of the garage, let alone beginning an endless search for my credit cards and license. I sat down for a second in the car to rest, pale and frustrated with the door slightly ajar.

My mom walked back to the attendant to discuss our predicament. We would need to leave the car parked for a while and go searching for the wallet. Surely, he'd understand. It wasn't our fault and anyway, I was a *cancer* patient in their facility.

"You paid for parking. If you leave and come back, you need a new ticket," he demanded.

"But I haven't even gotten into my car," my mom calmly explained.

"New ticket."

"We'll just be a minute. You see, my daughter lost her wallet. We'll just go run and find it," she countered.

"You must have a new ticket."

"Don't you see she has cancer?" My mom's voice was turning to a high shriek.

"I lose my job for this. **NEW TICKET P-L-E-A-S-E."**

In my 37 years of life, I had never heard my mother curse at anyone. She was raised in Brooklyn, NY in an era in which respectable young women did not have potty mouths. If extremely frustrated, the worst she'd blurt out was "nuts" or "crappola" Even if a large SUV were to roll over her little toe, the most I'd expect was an anguished "fudge." That day, she had reached her limit. The stress of watching her only daughter undergo hours of chemo coupled with the travesty of escalating New York City parking rates had pushed her right-over-the-edge.

"What a total asshole!!!"

My mom swung around, sprinted towards her minivan and hopped in.

"Shut the door," she ordered me.

I swung my legs around just as she floored the accelerator and zoomed back up the ramp. She parked again right before the sidewalk began, blocking the entire exit lane of the garage.

"Get out! Quick!"

She grabbed my arm and, together, we marched defiantly back across the street, car keys in her pocket. The attendant gesticulated wildly behind us. He yelled something inappropriate and incoherent. As we re-entered the expansive lobby, my mom concealed a Cheshire smile. Soon after I pressed the UP button, a vague realization materialized through the chemo-induced fog in my brain. I reached around for my mother's purse and slowly unzipped it. My silver-colored wallet peeked out naughtily from inside.

I'd like to say that we went back to our car and sped off to Westchester in triumph. We both deserved a win that day. In reality, I forced my mother to walk back down the ramp and to tip the extremely shocked and pissed-off attendant. I'd decided already that the rules wouldn't change because I had cancer. It kept me sane to continue adhering to social norms. I wouldn't stop holding doors for young mothers with strollers. I wouldn't skip the line in public bathrooms. I would wait my turn. The custom of tipping was too ingrained in me. I couldn't give it up, even for poor service providers or parking lot jackasses on my first day of chemo.

"The Dirty Dozen"

I fully admit that my default workday diet has always been a terrible combination of snacks and sugary drinks. Even during my first pregnancy, which coincided with a very tough year of residency, I mostly consumed Mountain Dew and Cheetos. I wanted to be healthier, but that junk was readily available in the vending machines at the hospital. In the past, I'd poo-pooed those individuals, such as one of my partners, Craig Zalvan, "a cheating vegan," who proposed that there was a direct connection between food consumption and cancer. But after my diagnosis, I was desperate to find some reason why this was all happening. Could it be diet-related? I had no idea, but eager to improve the situation, my husband and I made a tentative commitment to adopt a healthier lifestyle.

Effective immediately, I would convert to a veganesque-organicish diet. I would combat the toxicity going into my veins with super foods in my mouth. Eventually, the whole family would follow suit and we would replace our dangerous chicken nugget dinners with heart healthy steamed kale and quinoa salads. It was an excellent plan in theory with only a few minor hitches. Who was going to cook these non-microwavable dinners while the kids were starving and banging their forks on the dinner table demanding French fries with ketchup? The other problem was the state of my appetite at that time, which was dismal at best. A short time after starting chemo, I found that all foods tasted metallic and unappetizing.

Accordingly, I started losing weight. Though this would typically be an appealing side effect, I gradually moved into scary-looking-gaunt territory. My friends, especially the thinnest of them, tried to encourage me to eat more, but the only things that appealed were the comforting, highly-processed, carbohydrate-rich foods of my youth: alphabet pasta, canned cream of mushroom soup (weird I know) and imitation Bacon Bits (eaten right out of the jar).

While I munched voraciously on salad toppings, Alex had started stress eating halvah and large quantities of non-organic meat products. He is an amateur chef who can prepare a mean steamed vegetable dish, but there was too much on his docket already with work, the kids, and a dysfunctional wife. Via, our nanny at the time, was wonderful and wanted to help, but she was not an intrepid cook. She could do pasta and simple dishes, but there was no way she was experimenting with seitan and soba noodles. I was too wiped to try. So, with no one in the house to prepare the appropriate foods, I held off on committing to any major changes in nutrition.

During my second round of chemotherapy, my sisters-in-law, Betty and Debra, graciously offered to accompany me. Debra was my middle brother Dov's wife. She was already health-conscious and open to strict dietary modification, to prevent more cancer in the family. Knowing we'd have an abundance of time to kill during my Adriamycin infusion, I requested a nutrition consult.

Adriamycin, aka the "Red Devil," is a chemotherapy often used in combination with Doxorubicin to treat breast and other cancers. Its nickname is derived from its red color and nasty side effect profile which includes low white and red blood cell counts, low platelets, hair loss, and mouth sores, to name a few. It is very emetogenic, or nausea-inducing. It can also make your urine change colors temporarily. A rarer and more serious side effect is irreversible damage to the heart muscle which can lead to heart failure. This risk is increased if you later need radiation to the chest. If Adriamycin leaks, or extravasates out of your veins, it is painful and caustic. Therefore, it is administered slowly with repeated checks for symptoms of burning or signs of redness of the skin.

As the Adriamycin was being carefully dripped into my veins, a perky dietician popped her head around the curtain. Samantha or "Sam" was just exactly as I'd imagined her: petite, very slender, super smiley with a short haircut and cropped bangs clipped cutely to the side. Debra had her notebook and pen at the ready while I made my typical mistake of trying to commit it all to memory. Sam started slowly, not wanting to scare me right off the bat. She cautioned me to steer clear of extreme diet trends like macrobiotics. She quickly transitioned into a discussion of various foods to avoid, or at least to eat in serious moderation.

*"I'm not suggesting that you eliminate red meat completely. Just save it for special occasions, like every 2-3 months would be acceptable. Even then, **never** order an entire steak yourself, but maybe split a few ounces between you and your spouse."*

Obviously, she had never met my six-foot-three, 200-pound,

primarily carnivorous husband who came home like a starving bear most nights, unable to have a normal conversation until he finished a plate of fried strip steak mixed with beef.

Despite my misgivings, I continued to nod in agreement as she proceeded to emphasize the importance of avoiding the "dirty dozen." This was a list of fruits and vegetables with the highest levels of pesticide and chemical residues. Apparently, each year, the Environmental Working Group analyzes the Department of Agriculture data. The Group then acts as the grocery "Santa Claus," publishing a comprehensive tally of the naughtiest produce.

Apples made the list yearly because nasty fungus and insects like to burrow into this delicious fruit. To ward off this attack, farmers coat their crops with various pesticides. Other repeat offenders included cherry tomatoes, cucumbers, imported grapes, hot peppers, nectarines, peaches, strawberries, and potatoes. Even innocent leafy greens such as spinach and kale should be shunned if not from an organic source. It didn't end there. Depressing additions to the concern list included wine, coffee and chocolate, and all other items derived from ingredients grown in countries with lax regulations on pesticides.

I left Memorial that day feeling sad at the thought of avoiding salad bars and fruit shake trucks for the rest of my life. Still, I was enthusiastic to embrace a healthier lifestyle. I returned to Westchester with the grandiose idea of change on my mind. One trip to Whole Foods later and I realized how much this food revolution was going to cost me. Forget about the sheer inconvenience, organic food is damn expensive! Raspberries for $6.99/pound, my God. How strong was the scientific data, really?

Also, I couldn't stop thinking about my Bubby. When I

was a child, my grandmother was always encouraging me to consume large quantities of fruits and vegetables: apples, potatoes, and carrots specifically. She insisted that I eat everything with the peel intact and contended that it contained all the vital minerals and nutrients. Another assertion Bubby made consistently, although I wasn't constipated as a child, was that I needed the roughage from the peel to poop regularly. I grew up trusting my Bubby's wisdom as dogma. As it turns out, she was inadvertently poisoning me.

It is now proven that the highest concentration of unwanted pesticides is in the peel. In Bubby's defense, she knew nothing about potential carcinogens, neurotoxins, and trace pesticides. While she was raising her children, farmers were focused on increased productivity. No research had been done about the chemicals they sprayed on their crops. Also, by the time I came around, my Bubby was probably exhausted from decades of peeling vegetables. Remember this is pre-OXO era!

Armed with the new knowledge Sam had provided, I'd like to report that we turned our household into an organic sanctuary, but I can't. We made some notable improvements.

1. We started buying cage-free eggs which is annoying because eight eggs out of every dozen have blood spots in them.
2. We look for kosher organic chicken breasts, but can't ever find thighs or drumsticks, which are the only cuts the kids will eat.
3. I didn't completely ignore the evils of non-organic apples, so we've been purchasing organic. But, I seem to be throwing away a lot of rotten fruit.

4. We're currently 50:50 regarding berry purchases in terms of non-organic vs. organic. Well, maybe it's really 70:30.

5. We stocked the house with buckwheat and farro, but no one has attempted to cook any dishes with them yet.

My best personal attempts at healthy eating involved trips to Mrs. Green's Organic Pharmacy for lunch with my friend Tiffany. They have a great wheat pasta dish and cabbage-kale salad. I occasionally ordered a "Super Green" smoothie just to show off. It's tasty and for a while after, I really felt very green (at $7.50/glass). Driving home, though, I was already starving. I found myself stopping at Dunkin Donuts for a chocolate chip muffin and a Coffee Coolata. Hey, don't judge me. Rome wasn't built in a day.

Bitz-n-Pieces

Apparently, wigs are all the rage these days in Hollywood. Most of the actresses on the red carpet are wearing one, which is how they make their hair go from short to super long in the same day. At first, the idea of wearing a hairpiece sounded intriguing. I imagined myself like Julia Roberts with her short blond wig in *Pretty Woman*, minus the hooker part, obviously. Although I hated the reason behind it, I thought it might give me an opportunity to experiment with my look. I had worn long brown hair my entire life, except for a small snafu at age 14 when I mistakenly got bangs and a weird bob. That haircut looked horrible on me. I was so distraught that I made my mother try to glue my hair back on. Since she couldn't, that was the only time I ever wore a hat to school and it was only to combat seventh-grade insecurity.

Bitz-n-Pieces is a trendy Upper West Side Boutique overlooking Columbus Circle in the heart of Manhattan. Under wig categories listed on their website, they divide them into Medical, Custom & Ready to Wear, and Fantasy. I wish I was there to "party all night" and "feel like my favorite music artist," as described for the fantasy wig collection. Disappointingly, I was there for medical purposes. Betty, my oldest brother

Zvi's wife, made an appointment for me with a personal stylist named Ruby.

Betty, Debra and I ventured there after one of my early chemotherapy sessions. Ruby was a tall, overtly gay black male wearing heels and I suspected that was not his God-given name. He led me into a private area with chairs and large mirrors and handed me a glass of water. There, he introduced me to several styles of wigs made from human hair that were so costly, they each had their own names. Interestingly, every time I tried on a new style, he insisted I looked, "Fabulous."

Ruby encouraged me to choose something long-haired, reasoning, "you can always cut it later." Her name was "Brenda," or at least that's how I remember it. Ruby encouraged me to choose a capless wig in which the hairs are sewn to strips of elastic. This made it lightweight, comfortable and cool, supposedly. After my selection was complete, we discussed highlights and shaping. Suddenly, I wanted to get the hell out of there. I was creeped out by the row of Styrofoam heads with a variety of detached Asian, Indian or European hair being cut, colored and blown-out by their handlers. As I hurried out of the store, I had the impulse to make jazz hands...

On the upside, I left Bitz-n-Pieces feeling relieved that yet another task was completed on my cancer checklist. I was prepared for the inevitable hair loss up ahead. A week later when "Brenda" was all primped and ready, Debra was kind enough to pick her up. I placed "her" on a high shelf in my bedroom closet, so she would be available when necessary.

A bit further into chemo, after Via shaved my head, I retrieved my $2000 wig from the top shelf, anxious to try it on. As soon as I did, I was miserable. Maybe I wasn't placing it on my forehead correctly, but I wasn't comfortable at all. The part looked off, the layering was too feathered, the cut was too long, and the light base color didn't match my pale skin. Within minutes of wearing it, I developed a splitting headache. Instead of feeling it was "breathable," I felt claustrophobic under its weight. Ten minutes in and I was itching like I had head lice.

Many people wear wigs without an issue. Orthodox Jewish women wear sheitels (Yiddish word for wig) all day every day to cover their hair in modesty from the moment they are married. Beyonce, Katy Perry, and the Kardashians all love to sport audacious synthetic hair. My friend Marina's wig (more about her later) looked entirely natural, even better and blonder than her real hair. None of these people seemed burdened by pressure or itchiness. So why did I?

I think the problem dates to my childhood. I never liked anything on my head. According to my mother, even as a baby born in the dead of winter, I ripped off my hats as soon as she could put them on. I thought wig wearing would be different and I was mistaken. By then it was too late. *Bitz-n-Pieces* would never accept a return, especially one this customized. So, "Brenda" moved to the attic. I left her alone in the corner until months later when my cousin Elena picked her up and graciously donated her to another cancer patient.

Later, when I was getting sick of my headscarves and baldness, I tried wig-wearing again. This time, I wanted less of a financial commitment. So, my mom and I went to a specialty medical supply store in East Orange, NJ, that accepted my insurance. Juliette came along. I had the misguided notion that involving her in the selection process would demystify the concept of Mommy's wig-wearing. Since I knew I couldn't stand a full head wig, I decided to give it a go with the Halo, a hairpiece that fits underneath head-wraps or scarves or is attached as one piece to a hat. The woman at the store was knowledgeable and helpful. She pulled out a black baseball cap with straight, mid-length, mousy brown hair attached.

"Women like this for running errands in sweatpants or for meeting the school bus in the morning."

In the dressing room mirror, I looked more like a female assassin than a soccer mom. Was I being too critical of myself? It didn't really matter because as soon as Juliette saw me, she went berserk. She bolted behind a velvet curtain, wrapped herself up in the cloth and refused to open her eyes, sobbing uncontrollably.

She screamed, *"Take it off, take it off."*

I have never seen her go that crazy. After all the time the poor salesperson spent with us, I felt guilty running out of the store so abruptly without any purchase. But Juliette was inconsolable.

And that was the end of my wig-wearing experiment.

Synagogue Celebrity

It may be difficult to imagine for those who don't live in a Modern Orthodox environment, but every Saturday after morning prayers, the families in our town gather at each other's homes for Thanksgiving-like meals and group play dates. This is assuming that you are socially active and that people like you. Before cancer, I would classify us as about average on the popularity scale. Sometimes, we felt embarrassed because we had no after-synagogue plans. In those circumstances, Alex and I would skulk home alone, heads hanging low, masking our shame at being "invite-less" by over-involving ourselves with the kids and their stroller-snack controversies.

We were generally fine with our position in the community. We weren't the favorites. We weren't the losers either. At least I think not. If not for my illness, we'd probably have continued at status-quo, never climbing beyond the mid-rungs of the social ladder. But, once the word got out about me, our popularity skyrocketed. When I daringly chopped off my hair, shortly before it fell out anyway, we became the coolest kids in town! Soon, we were double-booked every weekend for lunch and our kids had their choice of playmates.

Interestingly, Alex's individual demand soared as well. Men

swarmed around him, begging to engage him in conversation. People who didn't know his name now banded around him like a phalanx. After all, he was the strong husband, the pillar of our family during such trying times. While Alex gained a new clique of guy friends, I became an actual celebrity. Women in town practically tweeted sightings of me in the supermarket.

"She looks good, better than expected."

"What a strong woman. It's a shame her children are so young."

"Spotted Tali in Stop N' Shop. Is that a new head scarf?"

Long gone were the days of social isolation.

I was the bomb.

The fall is a busy holiday season on the Jewish calendar, and it was important to me to participate. On Rosh Hashana, the lunar calendar New Year, I decided to brave the mob and attend the prayer services. I didn't feel up to being noticed so I stealthily approached the building from the less conspicuous side entrance (cue slow-motion music). Despite my best efforts, I was immediately spotted by my fans. At first, it was just a few friends who stopped to greet me on the concrete stairs. But soon the landing became packed with High Holy Days well-wishers complimenting me on my complexion.

"You look so healthy. I'd never know."

"Thanks."

I'm not!

The crowd gradually intensified to the point that children were left hanging from the railings. I swear I saw one woman deliberately elbow another in attempt to breach my inner circle of conversation. It was a brutal move but sooo worth it just to get my attention.

The difficulty with being such a cancer-fighting Goddess is that you inevitably become a symbol of women everywhere. I began to dread the questions and encouragements.

"How are you feeling?"

"How do you stay so positive?"

"You're amazing!"

I didn't feel that way. Outwardly, I maintained my well-dressed, put-together, makeup-always-on appearance. I smiled at praises and I always remembered to wear dazzling earrings. Inside though, I was slipping, retreating into myself. But I didn't dare let them see. In my darker months, I stopped going to Synagogue altogether. I couldn't bear the pressure of keeping up a brave face. I stopped applying my eyebrows and gluing my eyelashes. I couldn't fake my perfectly-lined-lipstick-smile any longer.

With time and practice, I learned to navigate and embrace the dichotomy. I realized that projecting courage may not reveal the whole truth, but it's not always a lie either. Best friends from high school, had seen me curled up on the couch, wearing the same ratty sweatshirt and scrub pants for days. They witnessed my fear and vulnerability and there was no shame in that either. Eventually, as the fall months passed, I regained my courage, too. I still had fight in me. I still had style and many more striking earrings to wear. So, I saved the naked truth for a handful of my trusted few. And for the rest, I picked out my red suede boots and re-emerged boldly as the Synagogue rock star.

Tripping in the Sukkah

One of the very few perks of going through the torture of chemotherapy, while not caring for any patients, is the license to ingest or inhale marijuana. In addition to the weekly meals of meatballs and mac n' cheese for my kids, members of the community offered to bring various other "baked" goods. My third round of Adriamycin and Cytoxan was on a Monday, three days before the important Jewish fast day of Yom Kippur, the Day of Atonement. Afterwards, I was horribly nauseated. The Zofran wasn't cutting it and the Compazine was making me constipated and drowsy. I was really struggling.

I wanted to attend synagogue the next day and needed some relief. That evening, my friend's husband stopped by to drop off a bag of "special" cookies baked just for me. His instructions were: eat half a cookie, wait half an hour for an effect, and if insufficient, eat the other half. I complied with his dosage recommendation as if it were prescribed by a physician. After thirty minutes, nothing was happening. As directed, I stuffed the remaining half in my mouth before going upstairs to watch tv. Forty-five minutes later, I completely forgot about the cookie but started to notice that the right side of my face felt numb. While watching *Old School*, I incidentally noted that

Will Ferrell was streaking naked down fraternity row through the television and right into my bedroom.

"That's odd," I exclaimed aloud. No one seemed to hear me. Soon, I noticed that my entire body was tingling.

Over the next hour, I very slowly made my way from my bedroom upstairs all the way down to the basement office where Alex was working at his computer. I held onto the banister tightly with both hands, feeling gigantic as I floated down the staircase.

"Am I yelling?" I screamed at him while his face faded in and out of focus.

When I reached him, I sat down on his lap and spun in circles on his wheeling chair.

Yippee!!!!!

This went way beyond taking the edge off. My sweet and ever-supportive husband laughed with me and told me to let go and enjoy myself. He was right. I had been living under the harsh light of reality for the past nine weeks and I needed a break. Due to the potency of the cookie, I didn't return to normal until 4 am the next morning. When I did, I was glad to feel like me again, but with sobriety came that familiar unpleasant feeling in the pit of my stomach. This experience taught me that it's all about careful titration. One-eighth of a cookie and I'll be warm and fuzzy all over. A whole cookie and I'll be on your rooftop, topless, believing I can fly.

Thanks to a thoughtful out-of-state friend, I acquired a pot stash in my spare freezer sizeable enough to get me arrested for intention to distribute. The goods were tucked surreptitiously between the freeze pops and the frozen broccoli. It was touching how many of my rather straight-laced friends offered to smoke with me in solidarity. I didn't mind sharing because I had no intention of needing it beyond chemotherapy. Despite my newfound access, my living situation presented a few challenges.

The problem with smoking weed in a small house with small children is the smell. Though you may think the solution is to just go outside, our backyard posed its own unique dilemma. It was a square postage stamp of a lawn bordered on three sides by neighbors without fences. No privacy at all! That is why I was happy this round of chemo coincided with the Jewish holiday of Sukkot, the Feast of the Tabernacles. Strange as it sounds, on this holiday, observant Jews like myself construct an unusual structure called a "sukkah," or makeshift hut, right in our backyards.

The hut commemorates the period of homeless wandering that the Jews experienced in the desert thousands of years ago. The holiday falls out around September/October depending on the lunar calendar. For seven days, the sukkah serves as an excellent gathering place to enjoy leisurely meals with friends. Often, it remains intact until early winter because it's so much work to dismantle. That year, our sukkah doubled as an excellent place for clandestine pot smoking. Our kids didn't know where to find us, and the thick canvas walls effectively hid this activity from nosy neighbors.

The first four days after chemo were the worst for me. I was incredibly nauseated with nasty GI distress for which my prescribed medications did not suffice. I wanted to feel better, less queasy, less sedate and less overall crappy. Alex and I snuck out to the sukkah early, while the kids were still asleep. He handed me the zip-lock baggie retrieved from the downstairs freezer and shoved it into the pocket of his hoodie. We quickly faced two glaring holes in our plan: one, we both forgot to buy rolling paper and two, neither of us knew how to roll a joint. In a pinch, I remembered my new glass pipe, a gift from yet another thoughtful synagogue member.

Alex never partook. He was there solely for moral support and his dexterity with the lighter. Our morning ritual worked well until he went on a business trip. Without him, I had a hard time coordinating breathing with lighting so, mostly, the flame blew out before I could inhale. I tried to improve my timing while, in the meantime, the weather got damper. In the rain, I was too lazy to go outside to the sukkah to smoke. Still, I couldn't risk the characteristic smell in my home. I started dangerously dangling my head out of the main bathroom window. A troubling cycle emerged: every time I got the red embers going, I coughed and blew all the marijuana off the pipe and onto the green grass of my tiny backyard. Eventually, I figured it out. Until then I reminded myself, "This shit is expensive... need to cough inside."

Super Humans with Super Powers

I really wish I had never known Marina Berg. Marina is an ENT surgeon like me. She joined my residency after her program dissolved. She is a good person, and indisputably *one tough chick.* She's Russian-born, without an accent, having immigrated to the United States sometime during childhood. I ran into Marina in Chicago exactly one year after our graduation from residency. We had all flown in the day before our otolaryngology written and oral boards. These exams were the culmination of everything we had learned in our five years of residency and one year of fellowship or clinical practice.

My friend Scott and I had spent the prior two months together in the Penn medical library quizzing each other on all pathologic diseases of the head and neck. Scott, Caroline, and I were gathered in our hotel room nervously reviewing everything there was to know about squamous cell carcinoma of the tongue. Off-handedly, Caroline mentioned that she saw Marina in the lobby wearing a wig. Marina had told her about her recent breast cancer diagnosis. She said that this information was not a secret.

During her first year in private practice, Marina became pregnant with her first child. In the third trimester, her ob-gyn discovered a lump in her right breast which turned out to be an

ER-/PR-/Her2/Neu negative tumor. That's the bad one! While thirty-two weeks pregnant, she underwent a unilateral mastectomy that she later described to me as "pretty awful for a few days." Soon after she delivered, she started chemotherapy. Two weeks later, while still undergoing chemo, she was back at work, albeit with a slightly lighter patient load.

Marina was about to join us to prepare for the oral boards because she had barely practiced any case scenarios. Why the hell not, given all the extra hours she had free between work, her new baby, and a punishing chemotherapy regiment? Marina entered the room with her usual casual confidence while I was biting my fingernails down to the quick. We spent several hours testing each other. She had only glanced at the pathology section. I had prepared over fifty note cards. To no one's surprise, Marina passed her boards the following day without breaking a sweat. Her blonde wig looked perfect the entire time. She seemed unfazed by the fact that this was the most important test of our lives.

The reason I bring up Marina again is that when I first found out that I had breast cancer three years later, I immediately contacted her for advice. If anyone could tell me how to balance breast cancer, motherhood, and my hectic surgical schedule, it was Marina. When I called, she was very supportive and after that, we began texting frequently.

Me (in tears): "When will the post-operative pain from the mastectomy get better? I'm miserable."

Marina: "I don't remember the pain being too bad. Take a few oxy and you should be fine."

Me: "Wasn't it torture to shower with plastic drains hanging out of your armpits and chest?"

Marina: "Imagine doing that while nine months pregnant."

Me: "Did your expansion hurt like hell?"

Marina: "Expansion was easy. I actually kinda liked watching my breast grow each time."

Me: "Were you self-conscious wearing clothes with a misshapen boob?"

Marina: "I just stuffed my bra, so I looked pretty much normal."

Me: "I can't handle the wig. It's itchy and gives me a headache."

Marina: "After a while, I found it convenient. It was faster to get ready in the morning."

Me: "It's been six days since my third round of A+C (Adriamycin + Cytoxan) and I still can't get out of bed in the morning."

Marina: "You should try to go back to work to take your mind off things...makes the time pass much faster. At least it did for me."

I had turned to Marina as my perfect breast cancer guru. I thought she'd have all the answers and be my most valuable resource. In certain ways, informational ones, she was. So, why did I feel so bad about myself every time we talked? I realized that cancer patients are not created equal, nor are their treatments. You shouldn't necessarily compare yourself to someone else because you are likely to end up feeling rotten. Despite our similarities, Marina and I had different initial surgeries and different chemo cocktails. Also, her mother had moved in for several months to help with the baby and running the household. If Russian women are strong, Russian grandmothers are made of steel. Maybe that was the secret behind her invincibility.

There was one other thing, that I only discovered much later. On a pre-operative x-ray for one of my many surgeries, the radiologist reported that he saw a rib fracture. He called me to ask whether I had ever been in a car accident.

"No, never."

"Are you sure?"

"It's not exactly something you forget."

"Well, there is a healed fracture on your left fifth rib."

At the time, I was baffled. During my next appointment with Dr. Gayle, I asked,

"Could that big anchoring suture you used to create the inframammary crease cause a rib fracture?"

"No. I don't think so. It's possible your rib was fractured during the initial breast excision. It's rare, though."

"Well, that would explain the unbearable pain I experienced afterwards."

"Yes. I guess it would."

After that discovery, I limited my communication with Marina. I know she was trying to give me sound advice. There are just some standards mere humans shouldn't strive to achieve, like Gisele Bundchen and her bikini-ready body three weeks post-partum. After that, I happily went back to watching back-to-back episodes of Mad Men in my pajamas and staying in bed until noon. I accepted the admiration of my cancer-free friends and family members who applauded how well I was coping in the face of adversity. They viewed me as strong for merely opening my eyes in the morning. Lucky for me, they had never met the unflappable Marina Berg.

Going Bra-less in Public

Unlike Marina, I had a hard time figuring out how to dress my new body. Looking good with tissue expanders in place is not a simple task. It requires finesse. To clarify, tissue expanders are not breast implants. That is a piece of information few people know unless they, or their loved ones, have gone through reconstructive surgery. You may even be asking yourself, what are tissue expanders? It's a valid question. I'm not sure I knew exactly before I was getting a pair of my own.

Tissue expanders are misshapen, deflated plastic sacks that surgeons slip into the space where your breast tissue used to be. They are essentially a placeholder. They are inserted at the time of the mastectomy. Then, over the course of multiple post-operative visits, they are slowly inflated. While fascinating, this can be unpleasant. At the start of each expansion, a needle is inserted through the skin and saline is slowly dripped into the sacks over the course of thirty to forty minutes. The goal is to gradually stretch the overlying skin to create sufficient laxity to accommodate your permanent implants. The good news is that the needle doesn't hurt because the skin is still numb, but the pressure sensation during expansion is uncomfortable.

The visual end-result of maximal inflation is not so flattering. After the final expansion, you are sent home with two rigid beach balls surgically attached to your chest. Also, the shape of the expanders, especially when looking in a mirror naked if you dare, is quite unnatural. They have these awkward sharp edges that jut out like the corners of a shoe box. To their credit, they are quite perky. I mean nothing is getting these babies down! In normal clothes, you look like a boxy-chesty Barbie doll. Even in thick sweaters, they can really hold up. Though annoying, there is a convenience factor while the expanders are in place, especially in bed. When the nightstand was full, Alex could rest a piping hot coffee mug on them. Unless it spilled, I wouldn't feel a thing. Needless to say, they don't feel great to the touch. Also, the kids didn't like them. Locating a comfortable spot for their heads while reading a book on my lap was nearly impossible (for any of us).

The single incontrovertible advantage of the entire lose-your-breasts tissue-expander-reconstruction-ordeal is that you no longer need a bra. I mean you can wear one, you just don't have to. I know what you must be thinking: wouldn't everyone see? That's what I thought at first. The thing is that even if the breast tissue is removed and the nipples are spared, they are no longer sensitive to cold, which means you will never again suffer from an embarrassing case of "nipple-itis." Despite my nipple-sacrificing mastectomy, I was still convinced I would always wear a bra. Without it, I was sure to feel weirdly exposed. I, Tali, though born in the 70s, was a product of the 90s. I was sophisticated and respectable. I would never go bra-less in public. Like so many other things I have learned along the way, I, too, can be wrong.

The first time I ventured out without underwire, I felt a bit like a flasher, just as naked underneath, but not as creepy. Eventually, I began to warm to the freedom. Unshackled, I could channel the mystique of the Age of Aquarius ...with exception of the drugs and the mu-mus. During trips to the mall, I passed lingerie stores without even slowing my step. I felt liberated. I, Tali Aronoff, could pull this off. In addition to the psychological benefits, there were other practical advantages as well. You save a lot of time and energy on laundry and even more on underwear expenses. If nothing else, it's one less hassle to deal with in the morning. I'm not saying my plastic boob-spacers were perfect. They sure as hell weren't cushiony for kids (or husbands). They certainly did not feel real. But for some time, those girls were all I had to work with. So, I resolved to wear them with pride.

A Boo-boo in My Boobies

Okay, technically I don't have boobies anymore. You try explaining that to a two-year-old who just started earning about gender differences and girlie parts. A precocious toddler, Scarlett was fascinated with the details of my surgery from the minute I returned home from the hospital. To date, even Alex had never asked to see my scars. In contrast, Scarlett was never afraid to yank my t-shirt up and sneak a peek. She liked to announce in all public places,

"Did you know my Mommy has a big boo-boo on her boobies?"

"Scarlett, not everyone needs to know that."

"Why? It's true."

She had a point.

Despite our chaotic existence during my treatment, we tried our best to maintain the kids' normalcy. It was nearly impossible when Mommy couldn't carry them around anymore. When I initially came home, my entire chest was bruised. I feared their childish roughness and even their hugs. I was sure they would never adhere to the new limitation on full-Mommy-access. They were used to climbing me like a tree, so this was a significant deviation from our standard family behavior. To my amazement, the kids adapted. They accepted that the rules had changed and might continue to change without warning. Also, our nanny Via had carefully prepped them about being gentle. When I first walked through the door after two weeks of being away at my parents' home, the girls approached me tentatively. They softly kissed my hands and cheeks, hugged my legs and did not ask to be picked up.

I had limited range of motion and soreness in my left shoulder after the lymph node dissection. As a result, I no longer allowed them to yank on my arm as hard as possible to drag me in the direction of a coveted toy or snack. Again, they both surprised me.

"Swing me around, Mommy," Scarlett pleaded.

"She can't Scarlett. Mommy's arm is hurt," Juliette admonished her in her wisest four-year-old voice.

"When will it be better, Mommy?"

"Soon Scarlie darling, I promise."

"Ok, Mommy."

And then, that was it.

Over the next many months, my sweet, sweet girls also learned that sometimes Mommy was too sick to get out of bed at all. The door to my bedroom, never closed to them before, was often locked. During those hard days and nights, they respected my detachment and expected very little of me. Still, every night before bedtime, they dutifully marched into my room to give me goodnight kisses and tiny snuggles, never complaining that I had done nothing to care for them all day. I am sure between Via and Alex, there was much behind-the-scenes explanation as to why their once energetic Mommy was so changed. But I prefer to credit my girls with their awesome ability to roll with the punches.

Despite their naïveté, it's uncanny how much their inno-cent minds comprehended. Although we shielded them from the full seriousness of the situation, we also didn't want to com-pletely hide the truth. Even if I wanted to, I couldn't pretend that everything was ok. It's too exhausting if you can't be real with your own family in your own house. So, they knew I was "a little bit" sick and that I took special medicine that made my hair fall out. They staunchly believed if I'd eat lots of fruits and vegetables, my hair would grow back in no time. I never told them anything to the contrary. Consequently, every night at dinner, they would each bring me a piece of carrot or an apple slice and demand,

"Mommy, you NEED to eat this so your hair will grow back shiny."

Their sweet misconception promoted good eating hab-its. Why bother correcting them? Although less than three, Scarlett worried about me constantly. I could see the concern pass in her brow, in her quizzical expression, and in her intense hazel-eyed gaze. There was no fooling my intuitive "Scarlie-bee." Preoccupied about my paleness one morning, she asked that I buy her some doctor's tools.

"Just in case you need me to fix you."

I complied, but urged her not to worry.

"Mommy's doctors will take care of her just like I take care of my patients."

"Ok, Mommy, but I should really check you."

The following week when I was feeling much better, we piled in the car and drove to Nyack, to the Palisades Mall. As soon as we parked the car, Scarlett and Juliette insisted that we go to the Disney Store, *shocking* for preschool girls, I know.

Dazzling and alluring for children (it's like a mini-Disney World), parents are powerless against its charms. We found ourselves at the register with two shiny tiaras, an Elsa dress, and one proper Doc McStuffin's doctor's kit. Immediately after returning home, Scarlett scurried around the house gathering her other toy medical equipment. Then, she led me into the family room and sat me down on the couch.

"Feet up, please."

She insisted on giving me her most thorough check-up, carefully listening to my heart with her bejeweled princess stethoscope.

"That's good," she proclaimed then paused for a minute, contemplating her next move.

Next, she pulled out the blood pressure cuff.

"What's this called?"

"A sphyg-no-mometer. It measures blood pressure."

She wrapped the Velcro cuff around my wrist and pumped.

"That's ok. Seems normal."

For her last trick, she reached into her new pink medical bag and pulled out a single Dora the Explorer band aid. She hesitated, then placed it across the middle of my chest. Afterward, in her most serious grown-up doctor voice, she declared me, *"All Better."*

V for Vendetta

Despite my daughters' urging for me to eat my vegetables, I could not avoid the total loss of my hair. I was born with a full head of brownish-black locks so, until chemo, my scalp had never seen the light of day. In fact, as an Ashkenazi Jewish woman, I had spent most of my life paying for hair removal rather than worrying about its scarcity. When I first thought about losing my hair, I was intensely fearful that I might uncover an ugly birthmark or weird skull deformity that had previously been hidden.

When I cut my hair successively shorter, I tried peeking between the roots for signs of a gnarly mole or giant area of dry skin. I spotted nothing obvious. Still, I never had a sufficient view. As my hair started to fall out in patchy clumps, the anticipation was killing me. Anyway, I just wanted to get it over with because the in-between phase was super itchy. Also, I was shedding like a cat, leaving traces of my presence everywhere and constantly clogging up the shower drain. I knew it was finally time to shave it all off. I just had to see what was lurking underneath. I begged Via to do the honors using the only thing we had around—a Lady Gillette. The dull blade was designed for legs. But, at least she could use it in the privacy of my home.

To my great relief, I had a perfectly-shaped cranium. I worried about Alex though. He had intended to shave his head with me in solidarity, but he has a more Russian square-shaped skull with a high forehead (although thankfully no Gorbachevian birthmarks). In the end, we hesitated because of concern it might freak out the kids. We had explained to them that Mommy's hair loss was a necessary evil, so I could get better. If Daddy had no hair, what would that mean? Too confusing. So, Alex kept his hair. In general, I had never been a big fan of the bald-white-woman look. Despite my apprehension, wherever I went, people kept complimenting me.

Fully hairless though, eyebrows and eyelashes included, I officially started looking like a cancer patient. I began wearing a headscarf, mostly so as not to shock the kids. Also, the back of my head was freezing. And, despite the accolades, I didn't find my appearance flattering. When I peeked in the mirror each morning, my only reaction was "man I look scary." I started avoiding mirrors altogether. My only consolation was that, in addition to no moles, I don't have overly protruding or weirdly shaped ears. Those are particularly hard features to hide when you have no hair.

One day, I was having a casual lunch with my friend at an outside space in downtown White Plains. A random woman in her late 50s strolled past me and then did a double take. I assumed she was a patient's mother who recognized me. Turns out, we had never met. She crossed back through the courtyard and walked up to my table with a tear in her eye to tell me she was praying for my speedy recovery. That's a nice gesture lady. Why exactly? Perhaps she prays for all sick women, just to cover her bases in case she runs into one. I appreciated her arbitrary concern, but this unsolicited emotion is worse than strangers rubbing your belly just because you're pregnant. I mean, would you randomly touch another woman's abs at the gym? I think not!

Except for the people I saw regularly, I still hadn't shared my cancer-news with my wider group of friends. So, I donned my new Hermes scarf (courtesy of Shlomit) and engine red lipstick (courtesy of Chanel) and took a selfie in which I am clearly bald. I finally felt ready for my Facebook reveal. I uploaded the pic and under, "status," I put an image of a pink ribbon. Not subtle, I know. Even without an explanation, my post received immediate traction.

"Oh my God. I had no idea."

"You look awesome. Stay strong."

"You will get through this. I believe in you."

"You are so courageous. I love that you are still smiling."

My absolute favorite comment came from Rina Bochinsky, a distant friend from high school who I hadn't spoken to in years.

"Leave it to you to look as beautiful as Natalie Portman bald (I'm assuming in V for Vendetta). You're still so annoying."

Her combination of catty and complimentary jealousy was exactly the type of response I was hoping for!

I was feeling more like an older, uglier version of Sinead O'Connor. Rina's perspective uplifted my mood. I felt cooler, more bad-ass, like the gender-challenging role of young Sigourney Weaver in *Aliens*.

Reading my Facebook feed was a nice pick-me-up. Most messages were full of shock, support and a desire to get back in touch. Others offered to help in specific or non-specific ways.

Specific: *"Please text me if you need any specialist recommendations. I will help." (contact information included)*

Non-specific: *"I'm rooting for you."* (no contact information at all)

Specific: *I would like to visit you at your house. Tell me a time and I'll be there.*

Non-Specific: *Sad to hear. Wish we were more in touch.*

Many of my better friends had already heard something directly or indirectly through the grapevine. Others who considered themselves close but had known nothing were upset. In my defense, I never meant to leave anyone out of my misery. I just had a hard time figuring out the most efficient way to disseminate this important and upsetting information. I couldn't exactly call everyone from college out of the blue to say,

"Hey_____. Sorry, we haven't connected in a while. Let's catch up and guess what? I have stage 3 breast cancer."

Can we say **awkward**?

I was too old to tweet about my cancer or post a cool real-time head shaving video on Snapchat, mainly because I didn't know how. Email was too impersonal and group texting was too inefficient. Even after my online debut, I remained somewhat reclusive. My voicemail was soon full and no longer accepting messages. I had dozens of texts and emails left unanswered. I wasn't ashamed of breast cancer or secretive about the details. I was comfortable answering questions. It was just all too raw. I wasn't ready to rehash my story play-by-play until it felt depersonalized.

Also, it may have been selfishness. I didn't want to hear about the aunt or first cousin or friend of a friend who had gone through treatment and was doing exceptionally well. I wanted the luxury of feeling uniquely tragic and I think that's ok. While I didn't return most calls, I did listen to every one of those messages. It felt good to receive them and some of them, I even replayed. As time passed, I stopped licking my wounds and began to widen the circle of trust. I had to be selective. I already felt overwhelmed by the close friends and immediate family who demanded to know every detail. Not a terrible problem to have, I know.

So, I prioritized.

Old college roommates- yes.

Co-workers- mostly.

Great aunts or distant second cousins- depends.

Long lost friends from kindergarten- not so much.

In that image I posted on Facebook, Juliette is sitting on my lap and I am reclining in a large padded white chair. It's a bit fuzzy but you get the gist that I'm bald, etc. Funny thing is that most people mistook it for a sterile hospital setting. Really, we were getting pedicures and foot massages at Clio nail salon. Juliette was only on my lap because we were both soaking our toes in the lavender-scented spa bath at the time. That's why I'm smiling so much. I surely wouldn't have drummed up as much support if anyone could see the young Korean woman pumicing my heels. I knew the picture told a tiny white lie, but the cancer part was true. Any-who, I won't tell if you don't.

Pink Night at the Beauty Bar

For my first October breast cancer awareness month as a cancer patient, I thought I should do something special. My awesome friend Tiffany recommended a champagne and skin care event at our local Bloomingdale's called "Pink Night at the Beauty Bar." It was the perfect justification to buy expensive make-up guilt free while raising money for research. That night, I decided to go all out with "La Diva" illicit pink lipstick, a matching scarf and a cute black sleeveless mini-dress.

Once I arrived in the store, all eyes were on me. I felt like the poster child for staying chic through breast cancer. The covering photographer, a lanky woman in her 50s named Judith, kept following me around and snapping tons of pictures. Absolutely everyone else was stealing glances at the skinny white girl with the turban on her head. I pretended not to notice. Under the scrutiny of the public, I nervously downed two free Bellinis in quick succession. Beyond the subtler attention, several people walked directly up to tell me how bold and beautiful I was. Though I was sure it was the cancer-patient allure that had everyone's attention, I hardly knew what to say, having never been hit on by so many women.

Another upside: Tiffany and I got a ton of free stuff at the

Bloomies event. The sympathetic girls at the counters kept stuffing our goody bags with samples. It was like make-up trick-or-treating without the inconvenience of walking house to house in the dark. I now own tiny eye creams and tinted moisturizers in practically every high-end brand. I even have a perfectly-sized tote to carry them in. I just wish I had worn a bright pink or even fuchsia outfit. I could have looked more "cancer-proud" for my photo ops. At least I snagged some cute pink ribbon pins for my jackets. More exciting, Judith promised that I might be featured in *The Westchester Daily*. Ah, the perks of D-list fame.

It was great to have new makeup, but it wasn't enough to distract Juliette and Scarlett. These girls are hair obsessed! Juliette has this beautiful thick, mane-like brown hair with natural highlights (which I credit to my mother-in-law) while Scarlett has wispier, light brown hair for which I blame my mom. Over the years their daily hairdos, with matching ribbons and fishtail braids, had become our family trademark. It was really a phenomenon and not credited to me. This salon-level care was entirely the work of Via, who was a hairstyling genius.

At the end of the year when Juliette was three, her preschool published a photo book for each child. Hers was titled, "Juliette's Year at Chabad." It would have been super cute to see how her face had changed throughout the year from a toddler to a charming young girl. But you can't tell because most of the shots were angled at the top of her head. I'll tell you, objectively of course, that people saw those two smiling little girls and their ever-changing hairstyles and instantly melted. So, it followed that the loss of Mommy's hair would be a particular tragedy in our house. For months, every morning at some ungodly hour, I was awakened by the exact same question,

Enter Juliette or Scarlett...
"Mommy, Mommy, I need to ask you something."
"Yes, sweetie. What is it?"
"When will your hair grow back?"
It was like my personal Groundhog Day hell.

As I mentioned, initially I cut my hair in stages. I think it helped them adjust. They still hated the change, as most kids do. They constantly complained that I looked like a boy or a spiky porcupine. In the beginning, they begged me to make it grow back. Scarlett cried and hid her eyes whenever she accidentally saw my head uncovered. I was forced into a painful daily ritual. Each morning, whenever I heard them stirring in their beds, I'd jump out of mine and quickly tie on my scarf, which I left in the top drawer of my night stand. I usually had about a 30-second head start before they came bounding into our bedroom. It felt like I was in a rom-com about the dating scene, in which the girl runs to the bathroom, brushes her teeth, puts on lipstick and then silently rolls back into bed before the guy next to her wakes up.

Then one week, I took them to the high-end Westchester Mall to buy shoes for school. We headed straight to the Nordstrom children's shoe department. The salesman there was a very sweet, shiny-headed man. As he bent down to measure her foot, Juliette's eyes grew wide. She motioned excitedly and yelled in her piercing outdoor voice,

"Mommy, look! The black man is bald too!!!"

I turned beet-red and quickly explained out-loud that, unlike mine, his baldness was a deliberate choice. She didn't listen. We chose multicolored sparkly light-up sneakers for each of them for school. Five seconds later, they both ran off to look at the fish tank. Before we left, the salesman gave them balloons and stickers. The very next day we had an amazing breakthrough... somehow, the girls had jointly agreed to accept me as I was, bald head and all. They decided to no longer be afraid. So, at exactly 5:59 am the next morning, my bright-eyed daughters burst into my bedroom together and declared,

"Mommy you are still beautiful...even without hair."

Trouble with the Curve

If I were a left-handed pitcher, my career would most definitely be over. Similarly, if I were a competitive swimmer or pro-tennis player, I'd be screwed. So, I should probably count myself lucky. Thank God, I'm a right-handed surgeon and most of my surgeries don't involve many left-side contortions on my part.

While I'll never be an athlete, I am still a mother of three who needs to stretch around the seat when Scarlett drops her Dora sippy cup for the twentieth time. Since this always occurs while I'm driving on the highway with my right hand occupied, good arm flexibility is essential to preventing a full-scale toddler meltdown. These are the problems you discover only as they occur and the things no one warns you about in advance.

I'm sure my surgeon did list the big scary surgical complications like motor nerve damage, bleeding and the dreaded lymphedema. But he didn't detail the more practical, highly-annoying implications of post-surgical scarring like the inability to reach the top shelf to get the baby food or to grab a super sugary snack from its hiding place above the refrigerator. I remember asking Dr. Alexandra Heerdt, a world-renown breast oncologic surgeon,

"So, anything to worry about with the axillary node dissection?"

"Well, some patients mention they need to stretch their arm up over their head once or twice a day."

"Okay. That doesn't sound too bad."

Anyway, it's not like I had a choice about removing the cancerous lymph nodes. In the brief time before my surgery, I was so anxious to stop any further malignant spread that I would have agreed to almost anything, short of chopping the whole arm off with my breasts. Afterwards, though, I began to care a lot more about the physical implications. Immediately after surgery, I could barely lift my left arm. My shoulder felt tethered to my body like a marionette to a string. Simply putting on a coat was tough. How would I comply with the security scan at the airport?

I was told that my problem stemmed from the fact that my armpit wasn't fat enough. I'm not kidding! Apparently, women with skinny armpits have a higher risk of scarring after this surgery. Who knew? Since I couldn't do anything about that, I requested a referral to physical therapy. It was immediately granted. I started seeing Nancy, a therapist at Lawrence Hospital Rehabilitation Center.

Twice a week, I carefully drove myself to Eastchester, eager to improve my arm/shoulder function. I quickly befriended Yelena, the nursing assistant, who would always bury me under a stack of warm sheets when she saw me on the treatment table, shivering. After gently applying massage cream, Nancy would begin torturing me with stretches and left arm rotations in various seemingly-unnatural positions. Though painful, it felt good having someone working so hard every week to make me better. I just wasn't so good at working on me on my own. Undeterred, she dutifully printed out my homework assignments at the end of each session and re-instructed me on how to use my red and yellow resistance bands.

"Make sure you do your exercises," she'd call after me as I walked out the door.

"Ok. Will do. I promise."

Inevitably, I'd return the following week, shame-faced and avoiding eye contact.

"Did you do your exercises?" she'd ask expectantly. Before I could answer, she'd preempt me.

"No, no. Don't tell me. You're a terrible liar."

I spent months maneuvering into the rehab center's irregularly angled parking spots and being tortured by Nancy, then downing three Motrin after each session. Finally, our time together came to an end. Nancy encouraged me to continue with my exercises at home (yeah right) and wished me well. When I walked out of the door for the last time, I realized that I should have brought her a fruit basket.

With therapy, I progressed a long way from the early days when I couldn't lift my arm past 90 degrees. After months of work, I was down to more minor frustrations like still needing to get out of the car at the drive through ATM to punch in my code and grab my cash. Ultimately, physical therapy was not enough to unhinge me. Apparently, I had something known as "axillary web syndrome." This is when a ropelike structure develops, for unknown reasons, in the armpit after axillary or sentinel lymph node dissection. At the time of exchanging the expander for the permanent implant, Dr. Gayle surgically released the scar bands. This improved my range of motion significantly. I continued to struggle reaching for parking tickets or handing the gas attendant my credit card through the car window. I resigned myself that I would never be an aerialist for Cirque du Soleil. Instead, I settled for being a work in progress.

Therapists and Sympathy at Every Turn

Before cancer, I rushed in and out of doctor visits. I never had a primary care physician or regular physicals except those perfunctory exams mandated at the start of any new hospital employment. In those appointments, I didn't get personal. The closest I came to a long-term relationship with any medical professional was with my dentist, but most of our time together was spent in silence with my mouth numbed. After my divorce and before I met Alex, I briefly saw a shrink. It was mostly to give my girlfriends a break from my constant self-deprecation and frustration with the New York City dating scene. In more recent years, I cycled through several obstetricians. None of them knew me well because I moved with each pregnancy. Anyway, we mostly talked about babies and gyno problems.

During cancer treatment, all of that changed. I would flit around from appointment to appointment with multiple layers of nurses and therapists pumping me for information. I became so used to being politely questioned or commented upon, from the saleswomen at Club Monaco, "I absolutely love your headscarf. Where did you find it?" to the usually inattentive cab drivers at the train station, "honey, let me help with your bags," that I was insulted when treated like a normal customer. Even the waitress at Umami where I frequently cheated and ate sushi (despite it being forbidden during chemo because of the body's decreased ability to fight off the bacteria in raw foods) always brought me extra spicy mayo sauce and a free pot of green tea.

Early in the expansion process, I followed-up with my plastic surgeon every two weeks. Later, I checked-in with my oncologist at the same frequency. As the phases of my treatment progressed, I converted to weekly visits with the radiation oncologist instead. I also started seeing Dr. Li, an acupuncturist, every Monday. Dr. Li was a pleasant, though not warm, Asian woman. She asked me each session, "What's bothering you today?" I realized that she was referring only to problems she could solve with the insertion of small-gauge, sharp needles into pressure points on my skin. But if I was feeling needy, I would elaborate regardless, knowing full-well that no matter what I said, I would receive her patented response: "It should get better." At least in her office, I was also promised a Zen-like recording of falling water and a restful nap.

Despite her penchant for torture, Nancy, the physical therapist, had been fun to talk to. She was a spunky woman about my age who looked much older and always smelled of cigarettes. While she performed her fascial release, I entertained her with stories of my nanny tribulations and crazy family drama. I interrupted my gabbing only to stop her from stretching my arm in a position which caused electric shocks to radiate down my left arm and fingers. This wretched sensation was likely due to compression of that pesky intercostal brachial nerve which may have been damaged during surgery. As a consolation, Nancy gave me green tea and ginger candies to take home with me. And of course, every other Monday, the chemo nurses provided me with free psychotherapy sessions while they hung new IV bags all around the suite. These chats were especially helpful because those women had seen it all. They perfectly understood all the awful symptomatology.

Even the most unforgiving traffic cops had my back. On the way to my niece's birthday party just before Thanksgiving, my Mom and I were tasked with picking up three large sushi platters. We were driving from Westchester to New Jersey and had been stuck in horrific traffic for hours. We were basically crawling. As per usual, my kids were going nuts in the back. When we finally arrived at the small shopping plaza in Bergenfield NJ, we were two hours late and super stressed. It was a long day and my Mom was driving. Abruptly, the car in front of us made a right turn into the exit lane of the restaurant parking lot. For inexplicable reasons, we imitated this illegal maneuver. We cut directly over the curved concrete edge of the exit into the lot. Two police cars immediately flashed their lights and pulled us over.

"*Quickly, uncover your hair. Maybe he won't give us a ticket if he sees you.*"

"*What? No, I don't want to do that. It's embarrassing.*"

"*Pleeease.*"

Before I could agree, my Mom reached over to yank off my scarf. Suddenly, my head was naked. I was still stunned when the policeman knocked on our window and peered into the car. He must have caught a glimpse of me, bald and slumped to the side, wiped from chemo that afternoon. After gruffly taking my Mother's license and registration, he disappeared for 10 minutes.

Even with the sympathy vote, I thought there was no way they would just let her go. We had literally jumped the curb past a clear, large sign marked "Do Not Enter" over a double yellow line right between the two parked police cars. When the cop finally returned to the driver's side, my mom was in a cold sweat. He was holding an ominous piece of paper in his hand as he bent down and peered at me one last time through the window. Be it compassion, the holiday spirit or just plain luck, he then ripped up the ticket and sent my Mom off with a stern warning to "never ever do that again." I'm guessing she never will.

WINTER
Christmakah

In the story of Chanukah, the Maccabees fought the Hellenists for the freedom to practice their own religion. Although the original focus of the holiday was on religious uprising and divine miraculous activity, most modern-day celebrations revolve around food and parties. American Jews have taken the elements of children's games and very modest favors of *gelt* (money) and transformed Chanukah into the giant Christmas-like, gift-giving orgy we are familiar with today.

My mother is the ultimate Chanukah Santa Claus. Every year she spends months purchasing, organizing and wrapping individual gifts for *each* of her children for *each* of the eight nights of the holiday. This generous tradition was feasible, though tedious, when she had only her four offspring to consider. Fast forward a few decades, one son and three daughters-in-law and eleven grandchildren later, and this task had become virtually impossible.

Nevertheless, she accomplished it masterfully each year, even without a team of elves or her own Amazon drone. I felt overwhelmed by the wish-list of my three children alone. I realized early on that I could not keep up with my mother, let alone with the current trends for my eight preteen and teen nieces and nephews. So, each year, I bought a stack of Visa gift cards at the CVS located just before the highway entrance. Then, I'd label them individually in the car. Four hundred dollars later, I successfully completed the gift preparation task while sparing myself the grief. Despite its expense, I still loved the holiday, filled with catchy tunes, golden chocolate coins and presents, of course.

That winter, however, I was not happy at all. Trying to celebrate the Festival of Lights is rough when you're smack in the middle of Cycle 4 of Adriamycin. I was flushed and dizzy, weak and fighting like hell to brush my teeth in the morning without puking into my pajama shirt. It was doubtful that my stomach could handle solid food, let alone dense fried potato pancakes. But tradition is a powerful thing. So, I chose a crisp white blouse and edgy black leggings to counterbalance my worn do-rag. Alex and I packed up the diaper bag and the girls and voyaged over the Tapanzee Bridge, headed to New Jersey for our annual family Chanukah party. The stress of three hours in traffic with one crying baby and two toddlers repetitively asking, "Are we there yet?" was abated only by the promise of warm jelly doughnuts and eager babysitter-cousins.

When we arrived, the house was abuzz with activity. In the living room, a beautiful array of school-child-made and bronze menorahs were lined up neatly on long clothed tables. The smell of fresh latkahs wafted through the air. The girls ran down the long, stately hallway. My nephews huddled together on the floor for a dreidel tournament with jellybeans. My nieces hugged me extra tightly. We lit the candles all together, even allowing the little ones to hold a burning candle, carefully. I leaned against Alex and tried to contain my overwhelming fear that someone's hair would catch on fire.

In the glow of the candlelight, I watched my father from the corner of my eye, burning his image onto my brain. I knew in my gut it would be the last year we'd celebrate together. We sang the ancient chant *Hanerot Halalu* about the miracle of the small jug of oil that burned for eight days.

"We light these lights for the miracles and the wonders... in those days in this season..."

My family sure as hell needed some miracles these days too.

Afterwards, in the kitchen, we milled about munching and chatting. Scarlett and Juliette were whirling around imitating the spinning motion of the dreidel. Amidst lively discussions of figure skating competitions, battle of the bands and slam poetry, I could almost believe that none of it had ever happened. My father was not dying and I was not sick. Everything was OK. I lost myself in that sweet thought for a minute as I watched all the cousins play together. Three yummy baked latkahs (thank you Debra) and one-and-a-half jelly doughnuts later I, mercifully, was not queasy at all. The holiday party was a resounding success.

Trying to make our escape before a massive meltdown, we changed the girls into pajamas and began loading them into the car with all their little teeth already brushed. We filled our sleigh-minivan with presents of puzzles and dolls, Princess Sophia paraphernalia and bags of new clothes. Alex and I smiled at each other optimistically, anticipating a smooth ride back home with peaceful sleeping children. I hugged everyone goodbye and kissed my father lightly on the cheek. And just when I thought I was in the clear... Scarlett leaned over and vomited **all over me!**

Stocking the Fridge

I have a shocking confession to make: I do not cook dinner for my family. I must also admit that, in the past, I had been rather complacent about what my children ingested during the day. From what evidence I could gather, based on the left-over morsels on the kitchen floor and smeared into the seat cushions, they often ate pasta with cheese and lots and lots of M&M yogurt. It followed that my medical condition did not significantly impact their daily food consumption. However, regardless of our actual need, we could not refuse the burning desire of the White Plains Jewish community to feed us.

In my town, the food making process for the sick, homebound and postpartum is a well-oiled machine. It even has its own website, "Take-them-a-Meal," and a complete email-driven structure organized by a busy local dentist, Erica Fish. In the beginning, I passively allowed our fridge to be stocked with various food items, most of which Alex and the kids ate and some of which would end up in the trash. I realized that I needed to become more selective. So, I started placing more detailed food requests with the communal powers that be: drumsticks, broccoli, and cauliflower OR meatballs with spaghetti (both girls), pasta with sauce (for Juliette) and pasta without sauce (for Scarlett). Milla was limited to baby food (please don't bother to bring).

For the next several weeks, every other day, we would receive a neatly packed bag on our doorstep. Inside, it contained several separate plastic containers filled with the exact food items I had requested. At eight weeks into the process, everyone remained happy. Via did not have to prepare dinner, the kids were fed, Alex had something to forage through when he got home from work and I was assured (for once) that dinner would be nutritious. Though I was tremendously grateful, I eventually began to wonder when the Aronoff soup kitchen would be closing its doors. Twelve weeks into the drumstick/ meatball/pasta rotation, my kids started involuntarily gagging at the sight of Tupperware. I was getting back my mojo and felt embarrassed at being handed a food delivery on my way out the door to TJ Maxx. Finally, Alex and I decided to put an official stop to the gravy train via a profoundly gracious email entitled "Thank you for your kindness...Now Stop." In the end, we left off the last bit and the message was warmly received.

From the outset, we had also been flooded with offers to help with childcare, shopping, and transportation to and from appointments. Betty set us up on this awesome website, "Lotsa Helping Hands." I could post any request along with the date and time by which I needed it performed. This solicitation appeared on an email sent out to my selected contacts. At first, I had rather lame ideas such as "need sprinkles for kids' ice cream," (too embarrassed to say they were really for me) and "craving Chinese rice crackers. Anyone going to Shoprite?" I dabbled in non-food requests as well. "Does Costco sell kids' bathrobes? If yes and going, please buy me two."

Betty thought I should kick it up a notch. Her suggestions: *"Can someone come scrub my toilets because my cleaning lady is sick?"*

"Anyone available to polish my hardwood floors?"

"Who can make Milla homemade baby food in assorted fruits and vegetables...no chunks please?"

Personally, I thought that was pushing the limits.

I also received many offers to take walks. This was initially my idea. I imagined myself home all day, bored out of my mind, too weak for any serious activity. I figured a daily jaunt around the neighborhood would keep up my spirits, so I might have mentioned it to a few people. Immediately, they started texting me with surprising frequency: *"Interested in a jog?" "Time for a stroll?"* I wanted to reply, *"Only if you bring caffeine."* My favorite walk was with my friend Jessica. The typical time we spent together was almost always in the noisy presence of our children and spouses. At my request one morning, she came over with a large coffee with skim milk and two sugars. We spent the next 45 minutes circling the block chatting about our husbands (probably mostly criticizing) and nannies and work politics. She missed several trains to Grand Central Station. It was worth it. The rare one hour of uninterrupted conversation was all we needed to truly deepen our friendship.

Eventually, I became overbooked and had to start refusing walk requests to accommodate my other social engagements. It got so bad I started avoiding people.

Her: "Standing on your driveway. You up for a walk?"

Me: (Peering out of my bedroom window) "Sorry, about to jump into the shower."

Her: (On another occasion) "At your door, wanna come out for a stroll?"

Me: (Fully dressed and about to go to Target) "So sorry, can't drag myself out of bed today."

Sometimes, I needed to tell bigger lies to avoid offending anyone.

Her: "Been knocking at your door to pick you up. No one is answering."

Me: (From the dressing room of Saks Off Fifth) "Too sick to even open my eyes."

Most of the time, if I didn't go out it was because I really wasn't up for it. There was a random unpredictability to my energy level that was hard to explain, even to good friends.

Some friends persisted no matter what. Despite my spotty communication over the years of medical school, residency and young motherhood, long-time friends, like my dedicated childhood bestie Bina continued to visit me like I was bed-bound in traction. It was very sweet, but I had become quite a commitment-phobe. I got it, I really did, schedules are tight, etc. I just couldn't promise that in three weeks from Thursday, I'd feel up to a social engagement. I may only feel good enough to sit on the front steps, or I might not want to get out of bed at all that day—let alone shower and get dressed for an in-depth chat about which of our high-school classmates had been most reproductively successful. On the other hand, show up unexpectedly at my door with *Life & Style* magazine, 80% cacao dark chocolate chips and juicy gossip about that girl we loved to hate in college and I was sure to open it.

Mocking the Grim Reaper

In my situation, I thought I was entitled to the occasional morbid joke. Apparently, though, I needed to be more careful about my target audience. My friend Ilana is a psychologist. Her kids are closely age-matched with mine, so my illness hit close to home. Like a lot of my newer Mommy-friends, there was a sense that if it hadn't been me, it could have been them. As such, friends like Ilana took my cancer diagnosis especially hard. She was very persistent about finding tangible ways to help. She sent me near daily status checks via email or text and was consistently on the volunteer meatball delivery rotation. And she's a vegetarian!

Once during my treatment, I mentioned to her in passing that I had fallen behind on birthday presents for Juliette's friends. The next Sunday, she sent her mother to Amazing Savings to load up on memory games and Connect Four. She delivered enough gifts to my doorstep to last me well into the next decade. Another time, we met at a fancy tea place in Scarsdale for pastries and a chat. As soon as we sat down with our scones, I casually mentioned that we were planning to move forward with our plans to build a home, even though, *"I might be dead by then. My odds are not that good!"* I happily slurped my blueberry iced tea with sugar-lemon coated ice cubes.

"Yummy, this is delicious. Is this brown sugar or white?"

By the time I looked up, her eyes were brimming with tears. Oops, too much?

I also needed to censor what I said around my sister-in-law, Debra. I love Debra. She is a thoughtful and caring human being. Still, I would not dare joke about death around her, even if I had a real zinger. In reaction to the recent double diagnoses in the family, she had already began converting her household into a hormone-free, organic, non-dye, non-processed environment. I wouldn't dare tell her that I might choose an early death over that degree of restriction.

Unlike my sweet friend Ilana or my sensitive-sister-in-law Debra, Alex can easily handle my morbid sarcasm. He's super cool that way and never fell to pieces even when I needed to verbalize my scariest thoughts. I must hand it to the guy... he doesn't spook easily. I remember when I first told him that I was pregnant. It was only weeks after we got married, which was also only six months after we first met on JDate. I had just given him the whole "it will take months or years to happen.... I've been on birth control so long" etc. speech when I realized that I was feeling a bit queasy. After a quick run to the drugstore, I walked out of the bathroom of our one-bedroom NYC apartment holding a pee-stick with two bright pink lines.

"Umm... I guess I was wrong."

He didn't miss a beat, just smiled, shrugged and said,

"Don't worry Babes, we can handle it."

Somehow, he's always had that easy faith in our ability to handle life's colossal stressors. Unlike me, he doesn't get thrown by adversity or paralyzed by fear. He goes right into adjustment mode as if it was totally normal that we just brought home a preemie-baby and now I might go ahead and die of breast cancer and leave him to raise three young children on his own.

"It'll be okay, Babes. I'm sure. We can handle it."

I really hope so because this is frightening stuff. But lighten up people! The Grim Reaper isn't coming any faster just because I say something mildly inappropriate about death or dying. Sometimes, it just makes it less scary if you put all your fears out there in the open and maybe even laugh about them.

Mommy is "Working from Home"

Years before my diagnosis, I wondered how all these women I knew were able to work full-time jobs while deftly running the household, cooking elaborate weekly Sabbath meals and staying abreast of all their kids' school related details... not to mention snapping up the best seasonal items at Costco. I automatically assumed that I must have inadequacies in the areas of organization and time management. I work five days a week, no exception, in addition to at least one weekend a month. As a result, I was always the delinquent parent. One time, while I was in the OR, I was called by Juliette's school to verbally give consent for the class field trip. The bus filled with thirty-eight kindergarteners couldn't leave the parking lot without it. This was after the third reminder had been safety-pinned to her shirt, so I couldn't miss it. And you can forget about chaperoning!

Once I got sick, I made a very interesting discovery. Many of the women I thought were working full-time in The City were covertly taking off every other Wednesday and half of every Friday. Their secret was revealed to me gradually and indirectly. It started with offers to take me to doctor's appointments immediately after my surgery when I was still unable to drive.

"I don't want you to take off from work," I would reply ignorantly.

"No problem, as long as I know in advance, I can work around it."

Well, that's curious. Great, thanks!

Over the course of time, I became suspicious of their consistently flexible schedules. What was I missing here?

I now know that this whole "working from home" phenomenon is a term many people apply quite loosely. For example, on Fridays, Alex's definition of working from home included multiple Home Depot runs and chopping vegetables for the chicken soup while participating in important international conference calls on mute. Lucky for me, his multitasking resulted in some delicious dishes while simultaneously resolving telecommunication connectivity problems in India. In contrast, my friend Beth is the most legit work-from-homer I know. She organizes the road shows for initial public offerings (IPOs) from the comfort of her suede couch. Despite her environment, she was razor focused and effective, and abided by strict coffee break rules and lunchtime hours. Nevertheless, she rarely changed out of her PJs and often managed to squeeze in a daily episode of "Ellen" or "Bethany" on the sly.

As a doctor, this whole working from home option doesn't really exist. Also, our house at the time was too small, and I had no designated office space, so almost nothing productive could be accomplished there. To train the kids not to bother me when I was on the phone returning patient calls or discussing hospital consults, Via often told them,

"You can't bother Mommy. Mommy is working from home."

In the past, this semantic tactic never fully succeeded. They continually tried to wrangle away my iPhone to look at silly videos of themselves while I was stuck on prolonged hold with the Westchester Medical Center patient transfer center. The strange thing is that after my surgery, there was a transformation. Even when I was in the next room, easily accessible but semi-comatose and nauseated, they did not bother me. I heard them giggling in the hallway,

"Mommy is in her bedroom. Yay!"

I came to realize that all they craved was my presence. They sensed that something was very wrong, but they were happier than when I healthily rushed to and from work like a tornado. At some point, Juliette told Via,

"I want Mommy to keep working from home forever."

I'm sure that in her heart, she understood that I was home because I was sick and really was not working. But, at that time, whatever brought her comfort was good enough for me.

Starbucks.... Where Everybody Knows Your Name

I thought of leaving an open credit card at my local Starbuck's. If I add up all the iced grande soy macchiatos I purchased since I got cancer, I could have taken the trip to the Galapagos Islands that I dreamed about. Instead, I spent all my time and money on what I suspect to be crack-infused flavored coffee. All this so I could rehash my sad tale with various friends. On a positive note, I accrued double mileage points on my Visa Venture card at an accelerated rate.

Typically, as I approached the green shirted barista, I was greeted warmly with,

"Hi, Tali. Will it be the usual?"

I felt the impending rush that only comes when you are about to indulge in a super sweet caffeinated beverage. My friend of the day would always pull out her credit card. A brief battle of wills would ensue, while the people in the line behind us became impatient. My super shiny Visa always won. I didn't like to feel indebted to anyone. After paying, I would make a bee-line for my designated seat in those comfy couches near the perimeter. This way, the fewest number of café-goers were trapped overhearing the intimate details of my life.

When we sat down, just to be polite, I always started with, "which version would you like to hear, the long or short one?" Then I'd press play on my mental podcast entitled "Tali's Battle with Breast Cancer."

I gave these coffee talks about a 45-minute limit. Otherwise, my listener's attention span started to wane, and my voice got raspy. For the most part, these outings were extremely cathartic, even when I was retelling how I found the lump for the 200th time.

Recently though, I went to lunch with Linda Silverberg, one of the few stay-at-home moms in my very working-women community. She has the pulse on all the current shoe sales and knows absolutely all the dish around town. Most importantly, she had selflessly driven my daughter Scarlett to preschool every single day since my initial surgery. She deserved a friendship bone.

Refreshingly, the first topic of conversation was not about me, but rather how our kids were enjoying school. To give some context, both her three children and my oldest daughter were enrolled in the same, expensive private, Jewish elementary school. On that day, I was expecting some opening pleasantries regarding the new principal and the wonderful teachers "Morah Lynn" and "Morah Joanie." Instead, she launched into a dizzying rant about how our school teaches "contextual" rather than "phonetic" reading. Apparently, as a result, many kids do not actually learn how to read by the end of kindergarten.

I was still processing this educational shift when she revealed that it wasn't until first grade that she realized her daughter did not know how to read. No problem, though. She enrolled her in the Sylvan learning center for another few thousand bucks per semester to augment the inadequacies of our schools' resource room. Linda warned me not to rely on the teachers to tell me if Juliette was having any problems and that I needed to monitor her progress like a hawk. Obviously, she had been in multiple meetings with the early education coordinator and had observed the classroom for a month in preparation for the upcoming parent teacher conferences.

"What do you think of Juliette's experience at the school to date? How is she doing in class relative to others?"

I was trying to catch up...they don't teach our kids to read in school anymore? I had naively assumed that my husband and I paid a staggering private school tuition so that, at the very least, our kids would be literate. How would I have known any of these things if not for the coffee talk with Linda? I tried moving on to less stressful topics like cancer recurrence rates and the scary long-term side effects of Taxol which include neuropathies such as tingling and numbness of the fingertips. How am I supposed to be a surgeon if I can't even feel my fingertips? But, Linda was fixated on the deconstruction of circle time. At this point, I was slurping the bottom of my coffee cup and wishing I had ordered a Vente double shot non-fat iced cappuccino, *with whip.*

In all honesty, though, these outings with friends were what got me up and going on those difficult days when I'd otherwise be hiding beneath the covers. Over $3 bags of mixed nuts and vanilla bean scones, I basked in the frivolity of casual conversation. When Linda finally paused for a breath, I got up from the table to throw away my cup. At the garbage can, I met a woman with cropped hair who looked at my patterned kerchief and told me "to keep fighting the good fight." I didn't know there was another choice, but I appreciated the encouragement.

Despite sometimes feeling under the microscope, I couldn't help but recognize that yet another friend had taken the time to come to support me through the process. And most conversations were not as informative or intense as the ones with Linda Silverberg. I did sometimes worry about the mounting cost of these daytime diversions, but Alex reassured me we that could afford it. Now, if only my gold Starbucks rewards card came with a malignancy discount.

The Nanny Dance

Let me start by saying I that love Via. She had been with us for almost two years when cancer hit. She was the reason everything functioned: Milla got her bottle in the morning, my older girls made it to school on time, lunch was packed daily, and I had clean underwear and socks to wear under my scrubs as I ran out the door each morning to the operating room. The one thing she specifically stated when we hired her was, "I only work for busy moms." In other words, she hated when moms were home during the day. This is a common theme among nannies and not a red flag that they are secretly smacking the children or sleeping on the couch while the kids play with scissors. After all, who likes the boss breathing down their neck all day, especially when the boss is a Mommy?

Up until Milla's unexpected early arrival, her criterion was not a problem. If anything, the bigger issue was that I often left before the kids woke up and got home after they were asleep. She literally ran the whole ship. I was only the weekend fill-in captain. My original intention after Milla's birth was to take about six weeks of maternity leave. For most, that's considered a rather short period of time to take off after having a baby, but I was determined to maintain the continuity of my patients' care. All my best laid plans went to hell when I suddenly developed preeclampsia at thirty-four weeks gestation and Milla was born tiny and premature, weighing in at 3 pounds 11 ounces. After her birth I gave myself one full week to recover physically and emotionally and went back to performing my previously booked operations. I had jam-packed my schedule right up until my due date under the misguided assumption that everything would go as planned. In the confusion of her hasty arrival, no one in my office had bothered to cancel my cases. I figured that while Milla was safe in the NICU being cared for by the vigilant nurses of White Plains Hospital, I could temporarily return to work. This plan worked until Milla was discharged home at a mere 4 pounds. I couldn't leave her and my two other toddlers with Via and run back to see patients. She needed singular attention. Frequently feeding her was a full-time job, so I was forced to take an extended maternity leave.

Despite Via's love of our new little peanut, she grew restless with my presence in the house. I tried to stay hidden with Milla in my bedroom, but I couldn't avoid eating or entertaining the parade of visitors who came to see our tiny addition. Via and I just barely made it through the extra four weeks at home together without her quitting. As soon as Milla hit a hearty 5 pounds, I returned to the office full-time. We all resumed our home routine for a short while.

Then breast cancer kicked my ass right back out of my profession and into convalescence in the tight quarters of our house. I did not want to violate Via's restriction yet again. In response, I went to extreme measures to make myself invisible in my own home. We had only one full bathroom for the five of us. Via had her own in the finished attic. My maneuvers were tricky. In the morning, I didn't leave my bedroom until the kids were off to school. I know that sounds strange, but this allowed them to continue their much-needed breakfast routine. Around 10 am, Via gave Milla, the most pukey-refluxy baby in the world, her morning bath. Often this coincided with my intense urge to pee, but I held it in until I heard the baby tub draining. Then, I'd wait for Via's footsteps in the hallway. At this point, I'd run to quickly relieve myself and brush my teeth. I hopped into the shower with my clothes prepared and hanging on the towel rack. Dried and dressed, I crept back into my bedroom where my computer and phone were located. I spent the remainder of my time trying to keep the noise level to a minimum, even whispering on the phone with my friends. I *really* didn't want to lose my nanny.

Though I didn't eat much, feeding myself was the main obstacle to my anonymity. I listened for footsteps indicating that Via had left to pick up Scarlett from pre-school before I went downstairs to grab breakfast. Typically, it was already noon, so even if I was queasy, I was starving. If I miscalculated and she doubled back into the kitchen to make Milla another bottle, I would wait in the short hallway in the back of the house. Occasionally, I got desperate and went down early to make a fruit shake. I had become something of an expert in shake-making because that was often the only food I could keep down during chemo on-weeks. Via loved them too, so I figured this endeavor shouldn't bother her. Even though I was temporarily encroaching on her space, she benefited from the outcome. I filled a large glass for myself, grabbed a straw and left the rest in the blender for her to drink. Then I scurried back up the stairs to my secret lair. Most days, I felt like a ghost haunting the upstairs of my house during the day and revealing myself as a human only at night.

A fundamental problem was that there was only one common living room/kid's playroom/laundry folding area. As a result, I stopped allowing friends to visit me at the house, no matter how crappy I felt. If I was up for it, I asked them to wait on the driveway and text me upon their arrival. I'd quietly slip downstairs and out the door without announcing that I was leaving. After a few months, I felt like I finally had the "nanny dance" down to a science. It was a crazy game to play, but all these maneuvers were worth it in return for stability on the home front. When I was physically ready to return to work as a physician, I needed to know that my support systems were firmly in place to enable it. Via only threatened to quit twice during that time, and that was when I was still a novice at being invisible.

Being the Doctor and the Patient

At the beginning of my journey, I felt very much like a physician and very little like a patient. Often, I found myself more than mildly irked that I had been demoted from Dr. Lando, a title which I'd spent a decade earning, to Ms. Lando-Aronoff, as it read on my insurance card. As time passed, I slipped more comfortably into the patient persona. I enjoyed sitting in waiting rooms, anonymously sipping ginger ale and talking on my cell phone while purposely ignoring the "no eating or drinking or cell phone use" signs prominently displayed on the wall. I started chit chatting with the nurses while they took my vitals, pleasantly commenting on their nail polish color rather than instinctively placing the blood pressure cuff on my arm myself or pointing out my juiciest veins for blood draws. In fact, I morphed so much into a patient that I was concerned I'd forgotten how to be a doctor. My female physician friends assured me that it was all temporary. I hoped they were right.

Typically, being a doctor-patient worked to my advantage. I often received professional courtesy, especially in the hospital setting. I was usually treated with more respect, which I appreciated. There were ways, however, in which my profession did not serve me well. I always felt obligated to solve my own problems, even when I was not in a good position to do so. For instance, immediately before Milla's birth, I was at risk for developing full-blown eclampsia. Eclampsia is associated with seizures, stroke, and death. Soon after my admission to the labor unit, I was placed on a magnesium drip. Twelve hours after safely delivering Milla, the drip was discontinued. Soon after, I developed severe chest pain. When I say severe, I mean Category 5 intense, heart-attack mimicking pressure in my sternum (breast bone).

After hours of watching me in pain, dismissed by the floor nurses as "normal," Alex began to rattle. At his urging, my nurse finally woke up the Ob-Gyn on call. She summoned me to the phone to describe my symptoms. Knowing that I was a fellow physician, though not a cardiologist, the on-call doctor asked me what I thought was wrong with me. I reasoned that since the pain was midline in my chest and not on the left or radiating to my arm, a cardiac problem was unlikely. I did not have shortness of breath, so it was also not pulmonary in nature. The most likely culprit was esophageal spasm or gastritis which, although not life threatening, can hurt like hell. I suggested she prescribe me an antacid and a sleeping pill. She wrongly assumed that because I was speaking so level-headedly, things weren't too bad. She complied with my medication request. She didn't know that I had been on the floor writhing in pain for hours before dragging myself to the phone at the nurses' station.

When Dr. Gardner called back a few hours later to check on me, I was sobbing incoherently. The pain had intensified. It was only then that the alarm bells went off in her head. She ordered basic labs and an EKG. Then, I was whisked off for the million-dollar workup: an echocardiogram to rule out a pericardial effusion, an abdominal ultrasound to rule out gallstones, and a CT angiogram to rule out the deadliest possible complication, pulmonary embolism. Only after every test came back negative, a strong IV proton-pump inhibitor and pain medications were prescribed for me. A GI consultation was scheduled for the morning. By the time the GI specialist arrived, my chest pain had eased into manageable discomfort. Apparently, it was just a horrendous case of reflux.

I had stubbornly learned no lessons from that recent experience trying to self-manage my medical care. Soon after my third round of chemo, I developed an irksome cough with some mild headaches. I assumed it was a sinus infection. Naturally, I prescribed myself Levaquin, a broad-spectrum antibiotic. I never bothered to tell anyone else.

I'm always uncomfortable when I call in prescriptions for myself because it is generally frowned upon.

Pharmacist: "Patient's name?"
Me: "Tali Lando Aronoff."
Pharmacist: "Prescribing doctor's name?"
Me (mumbling): "Dr. Tali Lando."
Pharmacist: "Wasn't that the patient's name?"
Me (indignant): "Yes it was...(jerk)"

Because I would never prescribe controlled substances, the pharmacists always begrudgingly fill my prescriptions. When my cough persisted for two-plus weeks, I changed my antibiotic. By this time, I was an oncology patient of Dr. Carolyn Wasserheit. Although I had received my first two rounds of chemotherapy at the mothership of Memorial Sloan Kettering in New York City, I soon decided that driving there every two weeks was too burdensome. So, I established my care at one of their satellite offices located at Phelps Memorial Hospital in Sleepy Hollow, NY. At the time I reasoned that this was more convenient while preserving my access to cutting edge clinical trials and tumor boards. Tumor boards are multidisciplinary meetings where complex patient cases are discussed amongst doctors in significant detail.

Still continuing to cough, it never occurred to me to call Dr. Wasserheit and describe my ongoing symptoms. After all, I knew how to treat a cough for God's sake, I was a pediatric ENT. At my follow-up visit the following week, Dr. Wasserheit asked me about any additional symptoms from chemo.

"Like what?"

"Cough, for example. Always call me about a persistent cough."

Apparently, inflammation of the lining of the lungs (pneumonitis) is a potential side effect of the chemotherapeutic agents I was taking. Drug-induced pneumonitis can cause shortness of breath, decreased oxygen and cough. The onset can be rapid, unpredictable, and occur as late as five months after therapy. It can be very serious and even lead to death.

Shoot, another bad judgment call. Luckily, at that point, my cough had resolved anyway.

I also appreciated being spoken to in medical-ese. I was extremely annoyed during one initial consultation when the oncologist told me he would just give me his typical layman's spiel. Insulted, I spent the next few hours brooding as I listened to him "dumb-it-down" for me. After all, I am far from a layman. Why did I bother studying all those years if not to understand the lingo? On the flip side, insisting on being spoken to like a doctor occasionally backfired on me. I was sometimes given the quick, cliff-noted version of my medical plan. Mostly, I just nodded as if absorbing every piece of information. I was often overwhelmed like any other patient, but I was just too embarrassed to admit it.

My very intelligent parents were better off for recognizing their limitations in the medical arena. They purchased a James-Bond-like recording device for all my father's doctor visits. It looked like a regular pen and wrote normally. Every time my parents met with a doctor, they'd each bring a pad of paper and independently jot down notes. One of them would have the special pen and surreptitiously press record. The craziest part is that they listened to the entire recording from each visit. They then summarized it in an email which was distributed to all my siblings. Despite their persistent urging, I absolutely refused to bring the spy-pen to any of my appointments. Aside for the chemo infusions, I would typically go alone. As a result, I never remembered anything my doctors told me. In hindsight, this is not a good idea for anyone. You always need another pair of ears and a good note-taker.

This lack of note-taking led me to mess up an important instruction. Neulasta is a bone marrow stimulant that is injected subcutaneously (in the skin) to boost the immune system. Dr. Wasserheit gave me clear instructions on how to use it. On the first post-chemo day only, self-administer one Neulasta shot. On the first three days, also take 2 pills of Decadron each morning with breakfast. In addition, she gave me a print-out copy of my chemo calendar which I dutifully taped to my refrigerator. She warned me that the injections can cause significant bone pain about five to seven days after administration.

The discomfort should be controllable with Motrin. She also mentioned that young, otherwise healthy people often have more significant and painful reactions because the naive bone marrow gets so revved up that it tends to overproduce white blood cells.

The CVS specialty pharmacy mailed me two boxes of Neulasta, a one-month supply and good for two full rounds of chemo. Each vial costs about $2500. Miraculously I am only charged a $20 co-pay. When the boxes arrived in an elaborate package from FedEx, I carefully placed them in the side door of my downstairs spare refrigerator. I did not trust anyone to touch these precious commodities.

As anticipated, I had an extreme reaction to the injection. On day five, the pain in my pelvis suddenly became so strong while I was driving that I nearly got into a car accident. I made it home in one piece, but the pain escalated to a point that I was calling my sister-in-law, Betty, for help. I could not sit down so I began walking up and down the block for hours. It was a feeling equivalent to the end stages of labor, which I had carefully avoided on three separate occasions with early requests for epidurals. Unfortunately for me, there were no OB-anesthesiologists randomly walking around my neighborhood at three o'clock in the afternoon. Desperate for relief, I took one oxycodone on top of the three Advil and the one Percocet I had already taken. Though still weary of narcotics, I was at the end of my rope. I didn't know what else to do. Finally, after about 40 minutes of wandering the streets, the pain began to subside. I returned home and passed out on the couch.

On my first follow-up visit after starting Neulasta, Dr.

Wasserheit's nurse came to take blood. At this point, drawing blood from my veins was about as easy as getting water from a rock; it required a bonafide miracle. This difficulty was a consequence of the harsh chemotherapy which had been delivered directly into my small hand and arm veins. This caused collapse of the veins which can last for years or forever. It was the result of a choice I had made: refusing a port. A port is a type of central venous catheter that is surgically implanted underneath the skin of the chest. It provides easier access to the bloodstream for the administration of medications and chemotherapeutic agents. At the time of my decision against the port, I was hung up on the scar. Looking back, it was a frivolous choice. That doesn't mean it was wrong. Back then, I was thinking about my neckline. I had always liked deep v-neck dresses and scooped-neck t-shirts. Facing such a big physical change from the bilateral mastectomy, I couldn't handle the idea of a separate visible scar near my clavicle. So, I declined the port placement. It was the only thing Drs. Gayle and Borgen recommended that I refused. Later, I paid the price by becoming "an impossible stick."

After my left lymph node dissection, I was prohibited from using the left arm for intravenous access or to take blood. Consequently, every time I required blood drawn, which was often, it took many tries, often by multiple people. It was also time consuming. If I was too cold, I needed to sit and wait for twenty minutes with a heat pack on my right hand to make my veins pop out. If I didn't drink enough water, I would have to hydrate, and then wait. Success was ultimately achieved only by the most seasoned phlebotomists, the best of the best, those who never missed. In one of my surgical pre-op visits, I had to draw blood from my hand vein myself because the nurse was so upset at the number of times she had tried and failed. She lamented,

"I just don't want to cause a cancer patient any more pain."

Maybe I should have appreciated her sensitivity. Instead, I was peeved. How did her sympathy help me? I needed the bloodwork. So, I reached over, grabbed the catheter from the table and stuck myself successfully.

The chemo nurses at Dr. Wasserheit's office were typically more proficient. After my first round of Neulasta, I waited for the results of my white blood cell count. It was 22,000, a number that is quite high, especially after only a single injection.

"Wow," Dr. Wasserheit commented surprised.

"That is quite a response. If this continues next time, we may need to hold off on the shot."

Cut to the next round of chemo, on day two... I slipped downstairs to self-administer my immune-boosting shot. The Neulasta box was mysteriously gone! Frantic, I tore apart the shelves and even emptied out the upstairs refrigerator, although I knew it was not there. Finding nothing, I ran upstairs and angrily blamed my husband, who in turn blamed Via for throwing away food and other items without asking anyone's permission. A few minutes later, from the depths of my brain, a hazy memory began to emerge. Perhaps I had taken the two Decadron, as instructed, on the first three post-chemo days. But I MAY have gone downstairs afterwards on BOTH of the first days for a Neulasta injection. It did seem slightly more probable than either Alex or Via recklessly trashing a container of important-looking medicine clearly labeled with my name.

I was forced to confess my humiliating mistake to Dr. Wasserheit. As for my mom, I never had the courage to tell her that she had been right all along about my need for the spy-pen. After all, I was a grown woman and a surgeon to boot! It was hard to admit that Mother still knows best.

Broken and Bald

In the end, despite my best efforts, Via buckled under the pressure of my prolonged illness. She didn't quit outright though. Instead, she surprised me by becoming pregnant. The shock at this news stemmed from two factors. She was forty-three years old with a grown teenager back in Brazil. She was also supposedly celibate, a devout Mormon who wore chastity garments underneath her clothes. I actually saw them in the laundry, although she must not have worn them recently. At her baby daddy's insistence, Via left us to marry him at my lowest, weakest point. This is how Vee came into our lives. Vee, formally known as Vimbai, was a 27-year-old young woman from Zimbabwe who had come to the United States on a tennis scholarship for college. We hired her without ever meeting her in person. During our two Skype sessions, I found myself apologizing.

"As you can see, I have no hair. I have cancer now, so it's a strange time for me. Normally, I'm not like this. When I'm better, things will be different."

Typically, I was the picture of female strength and self-assurance when interviewing new candidates for child care. Now, I felt vulnerable. Who was this weak woman Vee was meeting? This was not me.

Vee joined our family when I had no energy to give my children much more than hugs and kisses. She assumed control where Via had left off. She faced Scarlett's anger at feeling abandoned by a woman who had helped care for her since she was six months old. During bath time, I sometimes listened by the door of my bedroom to see how the children were adjusting.

"We do not want you. We do not love you. We want Via back."

It was a rocky transition at best, but Vee persevered. She earned their affection over months, with patience and time. In addition to the challenge with the kids, it really bothered me for her to see me as a weakling. But this was deep into chemotherapy and I was vulnerable and exhausted. At least, unlike Via, she didn't seem to mind my being around.

I was floundering, struggling with the loss of my identity. The swells of chemo didn't help. At the start of my next round, these feelings were boiling to the surface. I sat in the waiting room filling out the pre-visit questionnaire. I had completed this document several times before at each of my oncology appointments. It included a checklist of multiple medical symptoms. It is a mandatory section in all medical notes entitled the "review of systems" (ROS). Having always been completely healthy, I traditionally drew a long straight line through the "no" columns because checking each box was far too inefficient. At this point in my treatment, I found myself hovering over the psychiatric questions: "Are you feeling depressed?" "Having trouble getting out of bed?" "Having difficulty enjoying life?" Asking these questions to cancer patients currently undergoing chemo was a bit ridiculous. It's like asking a woman in labor (pre-epidural) if she is experiencing any pain. Shouldn't all the answers be "yes"? Sorrow was a rational response to facing a life-threatening illness. Wasn't it?

Until this point, I didn't really feel depressed, at least not in the classical sense. Of course, I'd been very sad to lose my breasts and really scared at my advanced stage of cancer. I had cried a hundred times for various reasons. So far though, each tear was in reaction to some really awful piece of news, a super painful part of surgical recovery or a crappy side effect of chemotherapy. All the tears I shed had been understandable, expected and not easily triggered.

From what I could tell, the onset of my deeper distress was sparked by two events. The first was a consultation with my radiation oncologist Dr. Randy Stevens, whom I adore. The second was my first visit to my ENT office since my abrupt departure four months prior.

Dr. Stevens is a wonderful physician with a phenomenal bedside manner. She is the Director of Radiation Oncology at White Plains Hospital Center for Cancer Care. She is caring and never rushed. She is dedicated to understanding each case and patient as an individual. I first met her by chance when she was a speaker at the "Pink Night at the Beauty Bar" event. During my initial visit to Dr. Steven's office, I received no new bad news, but she did elucidate in detail the overall treatment landscape. While I was grateful for the clarity, two pieces of information that she presented surprised me. First, radiation would last seven weeks, rather than the five and a half weeks I expected. Secondly, she warned me that approximately two weeks after the completion of radiation, many people experience severe fatigue. She explained that even though the treatment phase is finally, *finally* over, the overall toll on your body is so high that the whole system sort of poops out.

This low-energy period can last from two weeks to several months, depending on who you ask. None of this information should have been so shocking. After all, I was a physician with easy access to medical journals and textbooks. Even simpler, another internet search would have surely enlightened me. But up to that point, I had been purposely acquiring knowledge in small, palatable bites. That way, I only needed to digest one bad piece of news at a time. I could then dig in and plow through that limited period of pain or nausea as if there was no next hurdle to overcome. This had been my coping mechanism and it had been working just fine. Suddenly, I was faced with the reality of the long haul and I felt myself being nudged into the darkness.

On that same week, I brought Milla in for an ear exam and hearing test at my office located on Saw Mill River Road in Ardsley, NY. On busy days, I typically saw about twenty-five to thirty patients there every Tuesday. I arrived late and felt like an intruder for using the employee entrance. It was strange facing my staff. Everyone seemed genuinely happy to see me, hugged me and told me how sensational I looked. My discomfort escalated quickly. Gone was my familiar persona as the confident female surgeon, running from exam room to exam room, flexible fiber-optic nasopharyngoscope in hand, breaking only for multiple cups of Keurig coffee. In that harried life, I skipped lunch most days to fit in overbooked desperate patients who needed to be seen ASAP, often at the behest of a concerned pediatrician. I didn't even stop to take potty breaks, except of course during my third trimester with Milla when, despite her small size, she was squishing my bladder all day. Who was I now? I was just a nervous mom bringing in her infant daughter to be checked for long-term prematurity complications such as permanent hearing loss. More than that, I was a patient myself, timid and weak, slightly broken and completely bald.

I cried most of the way home. Up until that visit, I had been reacting to the problems I was facing in an action-oriented manner. If I felt sad, I called a friend or family member to unload. If I felt trapped at home, I dragged myself out for a walk. If I felt ugly or unattractive, which was quite often, I put on makeup or a new outfit. If I couldn't get out of bed because of wretched nausea or weakness, I snuck chocolate-coated marshmallows from my bottom nightstand drawer and shopped on Etsy on my iPhone. The problem with true depression is that you become awful at solving your own problems. Even the smallest challenge becomes overwhelming, no matter how simple and obvious the solution may be. For me, it was more a case of depression-lite. I could still smile and laugh at stupid jokes. I could still tickle Scarlett and enjoy her throaty cackle. I was just tearful frequently and for little reason. Now, I felt hopeless, staring at my calendar and the many more months of treatment that stretched out ahead of me.

I mention this because I believe most people undergoing treatment for cancer reach this same place. This is The Lowest Point. It is the depth you just cannot see your way out of when the waves are crashing above your head and you are drowning no matter how well you can swim. It is a critical juncture. It is the time to finally ask for professional help. Whether it be from your oncologist, a social worker, a psychiatrist or psychologist, the help you need is likely beyond the scope of a spouse or friend, however wonderful he or she may be at listening. You may need some pharmacologic aid, temporarily or long-term. The need to lift the fog and de-funk the funk is real. Do not think of this period as a time of weakness because it is a natural nadir to reach, facing mortality and suffering.

In my case, I was figuring it all out and weighing my options. I carried around multiple prescriptions for antidepressants in my wallet, but they remained unfilled. It empowered me to feel I could regain control at any moment. Still, I continued to ride the emotional roller coaster daily. When it dipped too low, I found solace in the knowledge that if I hit rock bottom, the only way to go was UP.

Funky Sleeves and Misplaced Belly Buttons

Without sounding too boastful, I will say that for most of my life, I had been complimented on my nice proportions. Be it height to weight, slenderness to curvaceousness, legs to body, I thought I was on target. I recently learned that it was all a lie. Apparently, my proportions were quite askew and parts of me were even un-centered.

Evidence of this problem first emerged while working with my amazing new physical therapist, Julie Lee. Julie is like a magician when it comes to breaking up scar tissue without a scalpel. She could knead the hell out of dough. After she went to work in my armpit, I felt as limber as an Olympic gymnast. Alas, that looseness only lasted until I left the building. She is also a lymphedema specialist. That day she was fitting me for a compression sleeve. A compression sleeve is a tight panty-hose like item recommended for preventing or controlling a condition of localized fluid retention and tissue swelling called "lymphedema."

Lymphedema related to breast cancer is caused by a compromised lymphatic system after axillary (armpit) lymph node dissection. To date, I did not have this condition, but I was always at risk for its development. I was advised to buy a compression sleeve for use during strenuous activity or flying because pressure change is a risk factor for its development. Believe it or not, there are various styles of sleeves to choose from, ranging from plain old nude to bold colors and even some that look like body art, manufactured by a company aptly called "Lymphadivas." Julie was taking a series of measurements of my wrist circumference and arm length and then ran off to print out sizing charts from the various competing compression sleeve companies. When she returned, I noticed her disapproving head shake.

"Did you know that you have unusually small wrists and disproportionately long arms?"

"Well, I guess, maybe," I answered with downcast eyes.

Julie proceeded to explain that due to my unfortunate limb sizing, I didn't fit into a neat category that would allow for easy online ordering. The only solution was for me to drive 30 minutes north to Rye Beach Pharmacy to enlist the help of a woman named Pat, a purported wizard of compression sleeves. Yes, there really is such a thing. Although clearly misguided, I had always prided myself on my long slender limbs and dainty wrists. It seemed everything about me was now under attack. I tried not to let it bother me. But, there's only so much a girl can take. It was hard enough being hairless and breast-less. Now, I was mismatched and misshapen.

I drove to Rye the following day, not knowing exactly what to expect. When I arrived, Pat was busy in the back with a customer. I waited for a while and eventually, a spirited woman in her sixties with short silvery hair, emerged from around the pharmacy counter. She introduced herself and accompanied me into a makeshift dressing room in the corner of the store. Pat enthusiastically donned bright pink rubber gloves. Kneeling on the ground, she squished my left limb into various versions of arm-Spanx while I pushed hard against her shoulder.

"You are one a tough customer, that's for sure."

She rummaged through her cardboard box, searching for my compression sleeve glass slipper.

"Voila, the perfect fit! Just make sure you wear it three hours prior to flying and three hours after landing."

Great, my next medical conference was in Las Vegas in May. I'm sure no one will notice when I arrive in 103° weather wearing a single long sleeve that looks like pantyhose sticking out of my cute sun dress. After she rung up my $45 bill, Pat sent me on my way with a smile, an extra pair of pink rubber gloves and vague instructions on how to shove myself into the arm stocking without her help.

A couple of weeks later, while I was still reeling from my visit with Pat, the topic of my physical abnormalities resurfaced again in Dr. Gayle's office. He was taking various measurements in preparation for my reconstructive surgery and enthusiastically drawing all over my skin with a purple "semi-permanent" marker. In reality, it would take days to scrub off that ink in the shower using a loofa as coarse as a Brillo pad. While measuring and scribbling criss-crossing lines across my chest and abdomen, he looked up at me with that familiar disappointed expression.

"Did you know your belly button is nearly one-centimeter off-midline?"

"No, but at this point, nothing surprises me."

"Here, let me show you."

"Oh, that's unnecessary. Really, I believe you."

But Dr. Gayle insisted. He demonstrated this disturbing discovery by dropping a measuring tape from my sternal notch to my belly button while shaking his head in dismay. He proceeded to pour over various breast implant sizing chart books, apparently searching for the ones that might correct my anatomical pickle.

"I think the problem is actually your chest wall curvature. It's off-kilter."

"I am assuming that's a bad thing," I joked meekly.

"Well, I'll do the best I can, but I can't promise anything. Best to have lots of choices for the OR, so I'll just order every possible option."

He continued to tick off a seemingly large number of boxes on the implant forms while looking far from satisfied. Being a perfectionist, he wanted me to know in advance that any subpar cosmetic results would surely not be due to his technical failings. Rather, my God-given lopsidedness would be to blame. That night, after my disheartening visit to Dr. Gayle, I snuck into my girls' bedroom to inspect them for previously undetected anomalies. Maybe these bodily defects were congenital! At their births, I remembered checking them for all the appropriate body parts in their respective correct numbers, ten fingers, and ten toes, one head, two ears, one nose. Yet, at the time, it had never occurred to me to bring a protractor to guarantee precision.

It was rather dark in their bedroom as I entered like a crazy anatomist. By the glow of their Dora nightlight, I could see their angelic faces resting gently on their pillows and their dainty arms and legs draped across their beds. In the sweetness of the moment, I hesitated to proceed. Surely it was insane to whip out the tape measure while they were sleeping, but I was in serious need of reassurance. When I was done with them, I crept into baby Milla's room, leaned over her crib and did the same thing... To my great relief, I confirmed that all three of my precious girls had adorably-shaped and perfected-located belly buttons.

The Michelangelo of Nipple Tattoos

I understand that cancer is awkward, especially when you are young. It's hard to know the right thing to say. There is so much variation from person to person. I admit that I was easily bothered. Even well-intentioned comments often made me want to rip off the head of the poor person who was just trying to be nice. On my worst days, a rather innocent, "well at least you seem to be doing well with the chemo" could send me over the edge of sanity. Another one of my pet peeves was being told, "six more weeks to go, that's not too long." Maybe not for you! Try having poisonous chemicals poured into your veins at regular intervals followed by severe fatigue, nausea, constipation, and diarrhea simultaneously. Then you can tell me if a month and a half flies by quickly.

Even my intuitive and very good friend Jasmine fell into the "seemingly harmless comment" trap. Before I elaborate, I need to explain about the two types of mastectomy: nipple sparing and nipple sacrificing. If the tumor is too close to the nipple, there is a significant concern that cancer has invaded the lymphatics. Therefore, the nipple is sacrificed because leaving it in place poses a high risk for local tumor recurrence. In nipple sparing mastectomies, the tumor is deemed far enough away from the nipple that it can be preserved. In both cases, the surrounding breast tissue is entirely removed. My initial surgery was scheduled as a nipple sparing mastectomy. This sounded great. I would get to keep the nipples I was born with even though I was losing all the underlying contents. Problem was, though they looked authentic, they were completely insensate. The advantage of nipple preservation is purely a visual thing and for many men, likely a sexual starter.

So, back to my Jasmine and her hapless remark. On that fateful day, I was sitting on her couch drinking tea, decompressing. I had just told her that I was having the nipple-sparing brand of mastectomy. She was visibly thrilled. Before I could explain the whole permanent numbness thing, she said excitedly,

"Thank God they are not taking your nipples off. Personally, without nipple sensation, I'd never be able to enjoy sex again."

Poor Jasmine, I know she meant that in the nicest possible way, but I shot back daggers with my eyes and blurted out harshly,

"Well, I guess I'm screwed for fucking then, because I will have nipples, but I won't feel a damn thing."

Jasmine's face became red. She fought back tears. I backed down and apologized.

"I know you didn't realize. Don't mind me, I'm just projecting my anger…"

Well, kinda.

In my case, despite the initial promise that I would keep my lovely nipples, my final pathology revealed that there was lymphatic invasion of the left nipple ducts. That meant, it had to be removed completely. Once the nipple was excised, there were various options to choose from:

A. Nipple reconstruction with skin harvesting (ouch and more scars)
B. Nipple tattooing (fascinating, but strange)
C. Do nothing and just live with it (not so appealing for someone in their thirties like me)
D. Some combination of A+B

The disadvantage of the first choice is that it entailed another surgical procedure. This plan sounded reasonable when Dr. Gayle described it as an inherent part of the multistep reconstruction process. Later on, the idea of yet another trip under the knife became a lot less appealing, especially if it was optional. Dr. Gayle's preferred method involved harvesting the skin for the new nipple from either the groin or buttock. This meant more scars and more discomfort and healing. Also, according to Dr. Gayle's nurse practitioner, Pam, he tends to over-project, creating "nipples shaped like bullets." Apparently, his surgical creations do shrink down to normal sized nipples over time, but the time course for this evolution is prolonged and unpredictable. In the meantime, one goes from the freedom of "bralessness" to the absolute requirement of double-padded protection. Otherwise, you look constantly aroused.

Another option involved nipple recreation with a local skin flap in which skin and subcutaneous tissue is harvested and rotated from a nearby sight to the defect. This option appealed to me in theory, but Dr. Gayle wasn't enthusiastic. He found that despite initial good results, the projection diminished significantly over time. The end result was often similar to tattooing. One of the most uncomfortable conversations I've had to date regarding nipples was with my mother. Understandably, she was tortured by the idea of all the surgical interventions I had to endure. She had been asking to come to a surgical appointment to meet Dr. Gayle. Despite believing that she was better off spared the details, I finally agreed. She was with me for the visit in which we discussed, in depth, the various methods of nipple reconstruction. Afterwards, we stopped for dinner.

"There is something I want to talk to you about. Please don't say, 'no' until I've finished."

This cannot be good.

"I want to donate my nipples."

"Donate them to whom?"

"To you. I don't really need mine and you need a new pair. It makes perfect sense."

Oh my God!

My mother's offer, while generous and well-intentioned, was obviously wrong on so many levels. The idea of having her nipples surgically attached to my new breasts was about as disturbing as that time a Jewish online dating site matched me 100% with my younger brother, J.J. Needless to say, I declined both proposals.

Worried about committing to new scars or bullet-nipples, I found the option of tattooing appealing. The downside of tattooing was that the new nipples would have no projection. So, not to be crude, but for the man in your life, there is nothing to suck, tweak or fondle. This brings me to Vinnie Myers, the "Michelangelo of nipple tattoos." Little Vinnies tattoo parlor is a modest establishment located in Finksburg, Maryland. Women fly in from all over the world to this shabby strip mall to have Vinnie, an amazingly talented artist, tattoo over their mastectomy scars the most realistic 2-D nipples money can buy. On the walls of his small waiting room, various areola portraits hang as a testament to his impressive skill. According to many breast cancer bloggers, this guy is the best of the best. His artistic nipples are so real, they can fool anyone visually, and it's only a few special people in one's life who will ever feel the difference.

Personally, I just hadn't decided which way to go yet. In my mind, I could argue it either way. But, I promised myself this... if I ultimately did choose to have my nipple-areola complex non-surgically inked, I'd only go to The Master. In case you're looking for me, be sure to check in Bumblefuck, Maryland. I'll be sitting there, sandwiched next to a bunch of sweaty tatted bikers in Michelangelo's waiting room.

Why Are We Talking About Nipples Again?

There is no way to explain the ongoing controversy regarding my nipples without being entirely blunt. As I mentioned, the invasive nature of my pathology dictated that the left nipple had to go. It was just a matter of deciding when to finish the job. None of my doctors wanted to delay the start of chemotherapy to bring me back to the operating room solely for nipple excision. On the other hand, no one wanted the nipple to remain in place, with its sneaky cancerous potential, throughout the entire course of my treatment. As a result, I was scheduled for breast reconstruction plus nipple excision during the small window between the completion of chemotherapy and the start of radiation.

Breast implants have an inherent risk of getting infected. This risk increases significantly in the setting of a compromised immune system. My surgeon wanted to wait until at least two weeks after the last dose of Taxol to give my immune system a chance to recover adequately. On the other end of the equation, the radiation oncologist did not want to delay radiation more than six weeks after the end of chemotherapy. The importance of this timing relates to the cancer cells' level of radiosensitivity (their susceptibility to being killed from the radiation) which occurs at a specific point in the cell cycle, known as the G2-M phase. Unfortunately, the surgical sweet spot for me fell out exactly on New Year's holiday week when practically all plastic surgeons take vacations, including mine. Consequently, my surgery had to be pushed back until he was available again, much to the chagrin of all involved.

This resolved the when but not the what of my nipples. In theory, everyone agreed that "lefty" needed to be sacrificed because of the concern over lurking cancer remnants. Now came the question of what to do with "righty." Dr. Gayle laid out two options, neither of which were appealing.

Option 1: Leave righty in place, sacrifice lefty and reconstruct the left nipple six months later. This sounded like the most appealing option because there was a 5-10% chance that I would eventually regain nipple sensation on the right side (At this point, I still had complete numbness in a wide band across my chest from armpit to armpit). The downside of this option was the visual mismatch that would occur between the native nipple and the neo-nipple that Dr. Gayle would proudly create. Righty had already migrated to an odd position as a result of post-surgical scarring. Let's just say that if Dr. Gayle matched the current position, the two "eyes" would be pointing out and down rather than staring straight ahead.

Option 2: Whack off both sides at the outset. Emotionally, I felt this was taking a step backwards. I had finally come to terms with the oddly shaped breast mounds created by the tissue expanders. Now, I would have to spend a minimum of half a year with two long matching ugly scars staring back at me in the mirror. On the upside, the end-product would be two beautifully symmetric nipples centered on my sprightly new breasts. From the male perspective, I'd imagine this to be a superior visual result. On my end though, I would have no hope of sensation on either side.

After laying out the options, Dr. Gayle told me to go home and digest the information. On the ride home from Brooklyn with my mother, I didn't say much. As was her nature, my mom felt the need to fill the silence. This time it was with painfully uncomfortable questions regarding... take a guess... my nipples. Generally, my mom and I are very close. We speak multiple times a week or even multiple times a day. I still consult with her on a myriad of issues concerning child rearing, home decorating and any range of shopping-related conundrums. I enjoy spending time with her and my kids obsessively love her. She had been my number one companion for chemo infusions and general support when I was feeling awful. However, the one arena in which I had no desire to involve her nor did I ever want her opinion was the intricacies of my sex life.

As soon as we pulled away from the office, she opened with,

"How are you feeling about the nipple problem? What does Alex like in terms of foreplay?"

I contemplated jumping out of the moving car rather than answering her question. We had only just started to accelerate, so I'd maybe break a bone or two, but I knew I'd survive the fall. I wasn't so sure about the conversation. Much to my relief, I was able to shut down her line of interrogation with an intense glare and an angry, "Mom, I don't want to talk about it!" My tone was that of a petulant teenager, but it did the trick and she switched topics back to clothes shopping. Phew! At least for now, the crisis was averted. The answers would come to me with time.

A Rack Like a Porn Star

At some point during the whole mastectomy/reconstruction process, every woman is faced with the difficult dilemma: what cup size should I become? In my case, I had started in my late teens as a solid 34C. I was overall pleased with my apportioned lot, given my thin frame. I was no Barbie doll, but I had sufficient breast-body ratio to satisfy most, yet too much to wear certain styles designed for flat-chested models. My "girls" had served me well throughout my twenties. Sadly, my thirties had not been so kind to them. In my five and a half child-bearing years, I gained and lost over 115 pounds of baby weight. This was the result of closely spaced pregnancies and their associated expansions and contractions. Also, many cumulative months of breastfeeding and hookups to breast pumps had taken quite a toll on my once perky boobs. Years ago, my friend Allison aptly described this as the "empty sock" phenomenon.

I'll admit that like many other women before me, I'd stood at the mirror contemplating what wonders plastic surgery could do for me. A little lift and tuck and slight expansion could improve the visual situation. But since no one on the home front was complaining, I knew I'd never voluntarily go under the knife. Plus, taxes, rising tuition bills, and household expenses had trumped my temptation to resurrect the bosom of my youth. No one ever wants to use cancer as the gateway to better breasts, but we play the cards we are dealt. Fate had intervened. Now, as I sat in Dr. Gayle's office with needles in my chest and saline bags hanging from the nearby pole, I had a choice to make: natural, big or even huge. What's a girl to do? The ability to select my new breast size was a rare moment in this whole ordeal in which I was able to dictate what I wanted to happen, rather than passively accepting my fate. This one decision was strangely overwhelming.

Here is a basic brief tutorial on breast implants. Disclaimer, although I am a surgeon, I am not a plastic surgeon. Therefore, my information was gleaned from web research and the patient experience rather than professional knowledge or expertise. There are two main categories of breast implants: saline and silicone. The advantage of the saline implants is that if they rupture and the liquid leeches out, it is safely absorbed into the body. Silicone implants are filled with silicone gel, which cannot be absorbed by the body. These gel implants feel more like natural breast tissue, but they need to be monitored more carefully. There is even a gummy bear implant. The idea behind this product is that they maintain their shape even if the implant shell breaks because the consistency of the silicone gel inside is thicker. These implants are also firmer. There are also various shapes of implants to choose from round, smooth and textured. Shaped gummy bear breast implants have more projection at the bottom and are tapered towards the top, which can become an issue if the implant accidentally rotates.

Dr. Gayle had shown me some samples of shapes, sizes, and consistencies of implants. Despite presenting these options, he had a strong opinion about which type would suit me best, and I followed his suggestion. Some surgeons also utilize computer programs called "breast implant animation" which enable you to see projections of the finished product. While this sounds cool, these animations are most accurate for regular breast augmentation and don't work as well in breast reconstruction cases.

Dr. Gayle recommended the gummy bear implants because he felt they would sit best on my oddly-shaped chest wall. He did leave the size selection to me. He cautioned me to choose wisely. Despite the encouragement of my well-intentioned female friends to choose enormous nature-defying boobs, I had to consider my end-game. The go big or go home mentality would likely result in much unwanted attention. Also, given my recent failed pole dancing experience, I was convinced that I had no future in the porn industry. I decided that a 38C rack on my size 4/6 frame may seem appealing to boobalicious Dolly Madison or Dolly Parton, but not to a respectable female surgeon trying to look professional.

I know I should probably have consulted Alex on this matter. He, too, had been struggling with helplessness. He might have felt empowered by the ability to decide on **something** about our wobbly future, especially since it directly affected him. What if his selection was recreationally fun but wildly inappropriate? In the end, I made the decision on my own and for my own reasons. I tried to choose judiciously, opting for realistic rather than original Barbie silhouette. It was a slightly augmented version of what God gave me, perkier and with a tad more cleavage.

Putting Humpty Back
Together Again

I ultimately decided to sacrifice both nipples for a chance to achieve symmetry. On the day of my scheduled breast implant placement and nipple excision, an arctic blizzard blew into the New York area with gale force winds and brutally cold temperatures. After slipping and sliding our way into Brooklyn at 15 mph, Alex and I arrived back at Maimonides Hospital in Brooklyn around 6 am. Suspiciously, even though practically every patient except me had rescheduled their elective surgeries, the hospital lot was still completely full. Alex dropped me off at the front entrance and started circling around the crowded snowy streets in desperate search of a parking spot. Inside the hospital, it was a ghost town. After Alex finally parked, we took the correct elevators up to the pre-operative area. I eased myself into the familiar patient hot seat, undressed and donned the required double gown. I felt older, wiser and more prepared. This was not my first rodeo.

Soon, the same litany of people began marching into my curtained cubicle. This go-round, I had to fake smile for no less than four eager medical students who happily informed me that they would be watching my surgery. I wanted to punch these smiley young kids in the face but instead only managed to be weakly authoritative.

"You do know I'm a surgeon, right?"

That comment created just the right degree of discomfort to send them retreating to the farthest point of the expansive room. A female anesthesiologist sauntered into my slot and introduced herself. I updated her about my previous post-operative puke fest, likely from the intraoperative narcotics. Concerned, she backed around the corner to confer with a colleague. They whispered behind the curtain and then returned together. Tehilla, as she introduced herself, offered me a "thoracic nerve block," an alternative form of analgesia to reduce the amount of narcotic required.

"It's like an epidural, but higher up."

It was a tough sell. Ten percent chance of lung collapse, awake for the needle part and not culminating in the birth of a cute baby. All in all, it sounded pretty unappealing.

"No thanks, just knock me out. A little vomit never hurt anyone."

This time, Dr. Gayle arrived exactly on time, having slept in the hospital overnight just so he wouldn't run into trouble with the snow.

"Everyone else cancelled but I knew you'd make it no matter what, so I figured I'd better be here too."

He performed another one of his abstract stripey masterpieces across my chest, a work I mentally titled *Potential*. I imagined it being drawn like *Harold in the Purple Crayon*. Mercifully, he made no further mention of my asymmetric bosom. This time I kept my eyes on Alex to make sure he stuck around until the last possible second. Before he absconded, I couldn't think of anything dramatic to say so I kissed him on the cheek.

"See you later, alligator."

"Catch you in a while, crocodile."

Back in the operating room, I went to sleep much more relaxed knowing I'd be waking up with a newly minted bust, albeit with no nipples. Everything went great with the surgery, but in the recovery room I could barely wake up. I really must have scared Tehilla the anesthesiologist about post-op nausea. I was so drowsy from all the anti-emetics she gave me that it took me five hours to safely get out of the recovery room. It took me another full day to regain my senses. By the following afternoon, I was finally back to myself, even though my body was taped up like a mummy. Since I was without drains this time, I could hardly complain. Still, the deep periosteal (layer of connective tissue enveloping the bones) sutures, placed to recreate the infra-mammary folds, hurt like hell. Not as bad as the first time around, but still not a cakewalk.

Seven days later, I peeled off the bandages alone in my shower. I eyed myself in the mirror skeptically. It took me a few days to gain the courage to cop a feel. Squishy, bouncy... not the originals, but they had a very realistic shape. Slap on some nipples and this could be an actual improvement from my pre-cancerous state. It was undoubtedly better than the sharp-edged tissue expanders. I was not exactly loving the enormous pink scars spanning each new breast, but given time, like the emotional wounds, I was told these, too, would fade.

Radioactive, Radioactive

Though I was still acclimating to my new "tear-shaped" additions, all my friends were anxious to admire Dr. Gayle's hard work. They also wanted to help me celebrate the short break between chemo and radiation. By mid-week, my lovable and clever friend Sharon had already sent out the Evite.

In bright pink letters, it read:

> "Come celebrate with Tali and her 'new girls.'
> Let's get radioactive before she does.
> 8:30 pm Saturday night
> Everyone, please bring something green
> to drink or nipple-shaped to eat."

The party was touching, and I was impressed with the creativity of the boob-cupcakes and appletinis. But, soon enough my hiatus ended, and radiation began. You know when you are breaking up with your boyfriend and every sad love song seems like it is written exactly for your situation? That's how I felt about the Imagine Dragon's song, "Radioactive," which was released about a year before I started radiation treatment. The songwriter, Dan Reynolds, once explained in an interview that the song was about the changing world and the empowerment of breaking free and doing something new. I found my own interpretation of their lyrics. The words played in my head on a loop while I lay naked from the waist up on the cold, hard surface of the radiation bed. Each verse resonated with me.

While Reynolds sang about breathing in chemicals, I had them coursing through my veins. While he was waking up and feeling things in his bones making his systems blow, I was falling asleep all day and no longer had bone pain from the Neulasta.

"Whoa, oh... I'm radioactive, radioactive."

I mean it's uncanny, right?

Radiotherapy uses high-energy rays to kill cancer cells. Prior to beginning the real treatments, you need to come in for a planning or "simulation" session. The purpose of this is to perform a scan of the area that is going to be treated in a position that can be reproduced precisely. Then, a bunch of physicists and dosimetrists, who you never meet, calculate how to deliver the radiation based on your needs and anatomy. During this initial visit, I was branded with my first ever tattoos. And, contrary to most people's experience when they first get "inked," mine was *NOT* cool at all. Rather than a charming butterfly above my ankle, my new tattoos consisted of several tiny bluish-black dots on my chest marking exactly where the x-ray beams needed to zap me to kill the remaining cancer cells.

Despite popular misconception, the radiation itself does not hurt at all. Each round lasts only a few minutes. But, man, those were some long-ass minutes. During the treatment, I was required to lie perfectly still. My problem was that my left arm had to be held outstretched above my head in a very specific position. Despite physical therapy and surgical release, this was the exact position I couldn't sustain. The residual scar pulled my arm down in the opposite direction. It took all my willpower to keep that arm up for a measly five minutes.

I started my radiation therapy at the end of January. In general, I was already a very cold person. I wore tights in my office in the middle of summer because the air conditioning in my building froze my legs. I was always worried that my patients would think I'm a total weirdo because while they come dressed in tank tops, shorts, and flip-flops, I was usually in a long-sleeved shirt and a cable-knit sweater. I justified my seasonally inappropriate wardrobe choices because most pediatric patients preferred a strangely dressed doctor to a stranger touching them with cold hands. As you can imagine, I am not a huge fan of winter. The only reason I like winter at all is that I can finally wear my multi-layered outfits without looking like a crazy lady. In theory, I should probably move to Florida, but realistically it will never happen because my entire family lives in the New York/New Jersey area.

Within seconds of taking off my shirt for the female technicians, I had goosebumps all over my skin. By minute one, I started shivering and my teeth began chattering. After precisely positioning me under the machine, the tech scurried off outside the radiation field and into the booth. She seemed terrified to see yet another young woman on the table.

*"Ok, Tali. Hold your breath and remain absolutely still. Concentrate. **DO NOT MOVE!**"*

I returned to my practice in the beginning of my radiation treatment. In order to make it to work on time, I needed to get to the radiation suite by 7 am every morning. The radiation sessions had to be continuous for five days a week. There was only a break on weekends. That meant that I had to be there every single day of the work week regardless of the severity of the weather. Somehow, the weeks of my treatment course perfectly coincided with several snow storms pummeling the New York area. Despite my frustration, I was amazed at the dedication of those radiation technicians. When every other office was closed for inclement weather, when I had canceled all my own patients, they still showed up for me every Monday through Friday for seven straight weeks.

I was finally lucky in that I did not experience any of the potential acute skin changes, burns, and breakdown that can occur from radiation therapy. This was despite following NONE of the special skin care instructions such as repeat aloe applications to keep the skin moisturized throughout the day. At most, I slapped on one coat of *Fruit of the Earth* Aloe Vera gel in the dressing room on my way out the door. Then, I bolted to work before the goopy stuff could dry. This, of course, caused my shirt to adhere to my skin like crazy glue. I needed to peel it off at the end of each day.

It was a hectic time, trudging through the snow in the darkness of the early morning wearing an Eskimo-like furry hat to cover my freezing bald head. Inside, I'd be chilled to the bone on the "tanning bed" of the LINAC accelerator. But there was comfort in actively fighting my disease. I reasoned that I couldn't be considered incurable until the cure was complete. Until then, I would continue to believe that the treatments were working and that my cancer dragon could be vanquished.

Sexy GI Jane

Purim is in March. It is the Jewish equivalent of Halloween, minus the trick-or-treating where children go around begging for candy from strangers in the dark, and with the addition of "mishloach manot," a tradition in which you drive around in the daytime with your children delivering little goodie baskets to people you already know. The dressing up part is pretty much the same for the kids, involving lots of princesses and Disney characters, but the adult customs are a lot less risqué. In our town, there is also a rowdy carnival held at the synagogue after the reading of the Megillah, the scroll containing the biblical narrative of the Book of Esther. At this event, all the kids sweat profusely while continuously jumping on huge indoor bouncy castles set up in the synagogue auditorium. During activity breaks, the children stuff their faces with cotton candy and popcorn. They continue bouncing until they break down crying, pass out, or someone gets elbowed in the face. That last part is what I always fear since I'm the only pediatric ENT in the building. The carnival is an insane zoo, but the kids go crazy for it. Adults with young children spend most of their time trying to ensure the safety of their offspring.

In keeping with the lively spirit of the Purim holiday, some of the grown-ups also don costumes. In general, this had never been my cup of tea and in the past several years, I had lamely gone dressed as myself in scrubs. This year had to be different. So much had changed for me internally, that it warranted an external expression. Also, I had the perfect idea of who to be: GI Jane! Given my hair regrowth, I was already sporting the high and tight military variant of the crew cut. More importantly, I already owned the perfect military outfit, or at least something close to it.

I had purchased this one-piece uniform approximately seven years prior, during my second year of Otolaryngology Residency. That year, Caroline, Avital and I were attending an exclusive Halloween party. It was set on the roof deck of my friend John's apartment in Alphabet City. I ordered the Women's Swat Team jumpsuit on spirithalloween.com. I was thrilled about the idea until it arrived in the mail and I tried it on. The outfit was just like the picture on the website in that it was a long-sleeved tight dark blue jumpsuit with the word "S.W.A.T" authoritatively displayed on the front. But, when I put it on, I looked fat and not at all awesome. So, at the last minute, Caroline and I ran to Claire's on the Upper East Side and bought matching sexy mailwomen costumes. We looked pretty smokin' at that party, but that blue cropped button-down shirt and thigh-high miniskirt were beyond unsuitable for synagogue. I wasn't sure what happened to it anyway. The jumpsuit, on the other hand, had successfully traveled with me through my many recent moves from NYC to Cherry Hill, NJ then to White Plains, NY. It most likely survived because it was still in its original packaging.

Due to the cancer and the chemo, I was super thin that

March. The little poochy stomach fat I hadn't liked in 2007 was long gone. I squeezed into the very form-fitting jumpsuit and was pleased. It wasn't exactly military issue, but it served the purpose. Outwardly, I looked confident. Inside, I was quite nervous. These were the earliest days of hair regrowth, when I was first starting to uncover my head in public.

After Megillah reading in the sanctuary, I walked into the main social hall of the synagogue flanked by my two older daughters clad in their traditional princess dresses and tiaras. My costume fell just within the lines of respectability. Alex came in behind me. I encountered a few of my friends' husbands as I made my way across the large room. To my eye, they seemed to nod their heads in approval. As a result, I began to loosen up. For the next few hours, I moved around the room checking on each of my girls at their respective activities. I received several more acknowledgements and comments, all of which I believed were complimentary.

"Cool outfit!"

"Ballsy."

"What a great idea."

"You look awesome."

I was sure that I had made the right choice. I put myself out there, despite my exhaustion and unsteady sense of self, to boldly represent Demi Moore as a female senator turned Navy Seal recruit. She portrayed the first woman to complete the most rigorous training course in the all-male U.S. Navy Special Warfare Group. In my mind, the parallel was obvious... strong female surgeon undergoing arduous cancer treatment, coming out successfully on the other side, etc. With this pleasing analogy in mind, I relaxed further and even to dared to smile. Eventually, I made my way over to the hotdog line. It was annoyingly long, as usual. It was already 9:30 pm and my kids were starving. I had no choice but to wait. Jon Rosner, my friend Dina's husband, was standing right behind me. The Rabbi stood immediately behind him. Jon tapped me on the shoulder.

"Are you aware of what it says on the back of your costume?"

"Duh. Of course, I am. Why?"

"No reason. Just checking."

Oh God, what does it say?

I forced myself to remain on the line and not to panic. My cheeks were flushed, but I needed to get those hotdogs and refused to retreat. Finally, I reached the front and purchased my food. Then, I darted to the women's bathroom and straight to the mirror.

Front in big white letters: S.W.A.T

Back in-giant-letters: Sexy-Women-Assault-Team

Fuck! Why didn't anyone tell me what it said on the back?

I slinked out of the bathroom moving my body flush against the wall and hoping to avoid another encounter with the Rabbi. I searched the room wildly for Alex.

I finally caught up with him shooting nerf bullets at a life-sized foam bullseye.

"What-the-hell? Why didn't you tell me what was written on my back?"

"You seemed so happy about dressing up. I didn't want to ruin it."

I was thoroughly mortified but I had a choice to make. Stay embarrassed and pissed at Alex or make it work. So, I grabbed a piece of loose-leaf paper from the Rabbi's office and Alex taped it strategically to cover the word "sexy". I walked back out with my head held high and continued to enjoy my night and watch my kids bounce themselves into oblivion. I did learn another important lesson: Next time I wear a Halloween costume for Purim, make sure to surveil all surfaces for inappropriate language.

SPRING AND BEYOND

At What Point do I Technically Become "A Survivor"

> *"I can't go back to yesterday because I was a different person then."*
>
> --Lewis Carroll, *Alice in Wonderland*

While I was still finishing up Taxol and my fingertips were still tingling, Alex once referred to me as a breast cancer survivor.

"Technically, Babes, I can't be a survivor yet because I'm still in the middle of treatment."

Although I had made it through the surgery and recovery and had withstood three and a half months of hard chemo, I still hadn't started radiation... and who knew if the treatment had worked? Who said I would even live through the whole ordeal anyway? Maybe I'd get neutropenic fever or develop some horrible infection and die. Unlikely, but still, I didn't want to count my chickens. Even if I flew through the months ahead, feeling great and without complications, what did that prove, anyway? I felt super healthy six months ago, when I was brewing an aggressive malignant tumor.

This leads me to the subject of surveillance. Until recent years, many oncologists monitored their breast cancer patients using tumor markers. Tumor markers are substances found in the blood that, when elevated, may be a sign of cancer recurrence, e.g. CA 15-3 in the case of breast cancer. For a period of time, the tumor markers are checked every few months. Rising numbers are considered 'bad' and suggest a possible resurgence of tumor cells in the body. Other surveillance options include yearly imaging studies such as positron emission tomography (PET) scans. Unlike tumor markers, which follow trends, PET scans are used to spot-check the entire body for recurrence. In the absence of a concerning finding like a new lump or changes in routine blood work, however, the American Joint Committee on Cancer (AJCC) no longer recommends either of these monitoring mechanisms. So how do you know everything is ok? It seems the answer is, you don't really. You just assume it is and go on living.

This lack of monitoring was a tough pill to swallow, especially with advanced disease like mine. Everyone kept asking if I was "in remission" or when I'd be legitimately "cured." Who the hell knows? I couldn't seem to get a clear answer on this point, not even from my oncologist. She'd only ever say,

"We're aiming for a cure. But, we have to watch you VERY closely."

The only thing I knew concretely was that the more years I was alive, the better... but my risk of recurrence would persist for a long time. Even my life insurance broker kept promising to "get back to me." So far, no company was willing to take a gamble on me.

I was scheduled to continue Tamoxifen, an estrogen receptor blocker, for at least ten years. Maybe this medication was just keeping my cancer at bay, but would I really be cured in the end? I will have lived another decade. I will have watched my girls grow to teenagers, start dating boys and driving cars. That's a good thing. But then what?

As time went on, I began trying to adopt a different perspective. Maybe every day, I was surviving cancer, even if I didn't have confirmation that it was gone for good. Each day I lived, I beat this disease a little bit more. I couldn't really say the words with conviction though. I was too scared to believe I'd ever fully ease back into life with all its small annoyances and daily challenges. I still couldn't imagine the day in which I wouldn't worry about my health. I came to realize that cancer treatment is tough, but, in many ways, the hardest part of it all is resuming life as if none of it had ever happened. Maybe you just can't.

First Steps

My journey back to my "normal" pre-cancerous self was not easy and is still ongoing. As I said, I returned to full-time work during radiation. For the first few weeks back in my office, it was challenging to acclimate to my role as the doctor. Patients noticed the headscarf after my long leave and asked with concern about the state of my health. It was hard to smile and say I was fine, but the reality is that no one wants a sick surgeon taking care of their child. I struggled through the fatigue, drinking 4-5 cups of coffee a day just to keep my engine running. Most days, I made it through my patient load on willpower and adrenaline, but as soon as I got home, I crashed. I fell asleep by 5:30 pm and, once again, my husband and children were left holding the shortest end of the stick.

At home, the kids did not adjust well to my reversion back to working-Mommy status. They were absurdly clingy whenever I was around them and anxious and upset every time I left. Even when I went to the bathroom, three little pairs of feet were always following just behind. With time, as I completed my cancer treatment "with intent to cure," I began to reconnect with the spirited young woman I had once been. Achieving full capacity at work took many months. There were also more surgeries ahead, though none as life-altering and difficult as the first. My scars began to fade but I still had weird ripples in my skin when I raised my arms. I was also a little underwhelmed by my size choice. My supposed 34C implant looked more like a B-cup and I surely could have gone more boob-tastic.

Slowly, like my energy level, my hair began to grow longer. The first several social events in which I sported my short, spikey 'do were huge milestones for us. My girls went crazy with happiness at the return of Mommy's hair, petting my head daily as it grew in. When I got some real length going, I dyed the tips and went through a funky rocker-chick hair phase that absolutely everyone loved... except maybe Alex. Despite my conservative nature, people now perceived me as fierce.

As time passed, I started to find my new normal. Unlike the period immediately after my return, now when my patients saw me for follow-up, they just commented positively on my cute, short hair.

"Thank you. This cut is so much easier to maintain."

I just didn't feel the need to explain anymore.

I still had hurdles before me, nipples to reconstruct, tattooing and defects to fill-in, but I woke up every day feeling a bit less afraid. I knew the future for me was still uncertain. I wouldn't be considered out of the woods for decades, which is a hard reality to accept, but I was keeping my chin up, hoping for new developments in breast cancer research and designing my new home with the conviction that I had a fantastic future. It may have been overly optimistic, but I was planning for my life ahead...

The Rise and Fall

Part of that life was a return to the structured routine of the Jewish calendar. By April, I had regained more energy and we prepared for the mighty holiday of Passover.

The Passover Seder is one of the most enduring and celebrated family traditions in Judaism. Even the least religious individuals gather with friends and family to eat matzah and retell the story of the Jewish people's exodus from slavery in Egypt. This yearly event forms the bedrock of cherished family memories. There are dietary restrictions on this holiday, paramount of which is avoiding the consumption of leavened bread products. The meal itself is like a wedding feast with multiple courses, often with 20 or more guests, including distant cousins and multiple sets of in-laws. As a result, the Seder is an intense affair involving massive preparation and set-up. Some people even have a mini-"Passover kitchen," where they can prepare Passover-friendly food weeks in advance. My mother has such a kitchen where she toils away before the holiday, much like the Jews did while building the pyramids under Pharoah's yolk.

My father's contribution to this holiday gathering had always been two-fold. First, he ground the horseradish for the Maror (the bitter herbs eaten by Jews at the Passover

Seder to symbolize the bitterness of the Egyptian oppression) and blended the ingredients for the Charoset dish (the sweet, dark-colored paste made of fruits and nuts eaten at the Passover Seder symbolizing the mortar used in the brick-laying in Egypt). Secondly, of paramount importance, my father had the honorable role of being our Seder emcee. His profound knowledge of the Bible and all other subjects, especially historical, was impressive and humbling and always commanded attention. The Haggadah, which means "retelling" in Hebrew, is a written guide to the Passover Seder. It includes various rituals, prayers, blessings, fables, and songs. My father had the ability to strike a perfect balance between rapidly reading the book's passages in ancient Hebrew while sprinkling in English commentary to explain the text when people became visibly bored.

My father had led the Passover Seder for as long as I can remember. That April was the only exception in his adult life. By that time, he had undergone a second surgery to remove a glioblastoma recurrence. While he had woken up lucid and sharp from his first surgery in the summer, immediately asking for his laptop upon his arrival in the neuro-ICU, this second surgery to remove tumor deep in the speech center of his brain had wreaked havoc on the most dazzling mind I had ever encountered. His speech, once eloquent and sophisticated, had become forced and halted. My whole family gathered at the large square table in my parents' finished basement, but my father could no longer lead us. He could still sit in his throne-like chair at the head of the table, but he could not stay awake for long.

It is difficult for me to accurately explain the scope of my father's influence on our family, our community and on his business world without sounding like I am blinded by my personal affection for him. But I know that the enormity of his contribution in this world is a truth rather than a daughter's perception. His friends and co-workers frequently characterized him as "the smartest man I've ever met," yet his brilliance did not come with hubris. He was approachable and curious and always learning. He understood me intuitively, in a way that made me feel safe and protected, even into adulthood. To witness his severe cognitive decline shattered the hearts of each of us in the family and, at my most vulnerable, it almost broke me into pieces that could not be rejoined. That Spring, our cancer-threatened lives crossed each other like a solar eclipse.

While he began dying, I was starting to return to the business of living.

It was the beginning of my new life chapter, the aftermath of surgeries and chemotherapy and radiation. It was the start of a series of hip-haircuts. I still felt tired most of the time, overwhelmed by my job and my children, but I was on the upswing. While I was regaining my strength and the faith that I would live, I raged at God for stealing his.

I think many of us find that when one tremendously stressful situation occurs in our lives, a second is soon to follow. This appeared to be the case for me. It wasn't just cancer + cancer. It had to be incurable brain cancer + metastatic breast disease. I remained standing because I was anchored by the needs of my very young family. Moving forward wasn't bravery; I simply had no other choice.

Beyond that, I had long felt that I was due for some sadness.

I had often worried that I was too blessed. My parents were both well. My grandparents lived long lives. I had never wanted for anything important. There was no poverty or psychiatric illness or even failure in careers in my immediate family. We had some divorces, disagreements and the like, but nothing lethal. I felt the cosmic force weighing on us, seeking to re-balance the universe. I'd had the luxury of too much love, too solid a family, and too successful a career. It was time for a reckoning. Although I was shocked by the seriousness of my disease and by my father's fatal diagnosis, I was not surprised that bad luck had finally come knocking at my door.

During that timeframe, people used to think it was com-forting to tell me, "God wouldn't give you more than you can handle." Well yeah, but it still sucks. Often this suckiness piles on top of you and you have no choice but to bear the load. To some outsiders, that will make you look like a surgeon-hero who managed her father's medical needs while battling her own cancer enemy. For me, being the only doctor of the family, it was the role I was obligated to take. My father had given me every-thing and never expected anything in return—until he became sick. Then he needed me to be his doctor-daughter-advocate and his designated translator of medical-ese. This purposeful role, while hard and taxing, especially in the toughest parts of chemo and surgical recovery, also saved me. It dragged me back to my life of utility, pulled me like the tide back to myself, my profession and my identity. And it made him proud of his only daughter, a fact that I would never trade, not even for an easier path in this world.

Deep Ravines and Laser Hair Removal

While concerns over my father's rapid decline occupied most of my worry, nagging annoyances kept emerging. On my drive to work in the morning, I secretly enjoyed listening to mindless talk radio, mostly tuning into the Z-100 Zoo. The hosts Bethany Watson and Danielle Monaro were always talking about "Ideal Image Laser Hair Removal." Between Christmas and Easter, they ramp up the advertisements, offering 99% discounts and endlessly pressuring listeners to be properly groomed for the holidays. These commercials were aired so frequently, that I had no choice but to remember that if I wanted to take advantage of the sale, I must call 1-800-Be-Ideal immediately. That's 1-800-Be-Ideal or Idealimage.com. Sadly, I never took them up on their offer. During my treatment phase, it felt like the women of the Z-100 Morning Show were taunting me. I'll explain why...

During my single dating years, I was rigorous about body hair removal, but I'd always stuck to the painful tradition of waxing. I was smart enough to calculate that I shelled out thousands of dollars in $80 increments over the decades. Yet I never acquiesced to spend hundreds of dollars for laser treatments. Like most others, I despised the torture sessions with the various estheticians who seemed to make fun of me in their native tongue. Still, I pushed off my big purchase for a future day when I would have unlimited funds to splurge on personal hygiene, i.e. never. The removal process was too darn time-consuming, involving multiple trips to a spa facility for the sole purpose of eliminating my hirsutism. By the time I had the proper funds, I didn't feel the urgency anymore. I was already married and not as eager to impress (sorry, Alex). Like many other things in life, it never occurred to me that I might lose my opportunity altogether.

Reasons I REALLY Wish I Had Pursued Full-Body Laser Hair Removal Before BRCA (And taken advantage of the discount)

1. As a surgeon, I felt very self-conscious being naked on the operating table. I was bothered by the idea that my body would be on display and people might think, "Hey, if she's such a smart gal, why didn't she prepare better for this." I know this is a ridiculous sentiment. No one in that operating room cared about my body hair except for me. Also, everyone was too busy focusing on how to excise the cancer that could kill me to notice that I'd been a bit lazy about grooming. Still, that thought drove me crazy. So, in addition to the required pre-op testing and chest x-ray, I made sure to coordinate waxing appointments with each of my four surgery dates. It was one of the most difficult tasks to complete.

2. The skin of the inner thigh is a common donor site used for reconstruction of the new nipple-areolar complex. The problem for me is that, without intervention, this bikini-area skin is heavily hair-bearing. Pam, Dr. Gayle's seasoned Physician's Assistant, swore that she'd be meticulous about removing all hair follicles from the skin graft during surgery. Nonetheless, I couldn't help imagining the messy result if she got a little careless on the day of my surgery or maybe lost a contact. I'm guessing the problem would only be noticeable weeks later after it was already too late.

3. The whole six-week, post-mastectomy, no-pit-shaving thing was an extremely unpleasant ordeal. It could have been avoided if I had better foresight.

4. A very strange by-product of my mastectomy + lymphatic node dissection was the creation of a new, excessively deep left armpit which is impossible to shave with conventional razor heads. No one ever talked to me about this particular post-surgical phenomenon or its' implications in the shower. Every time I saw my surgeon, I was so distracted by more important things that I'd forget to ask him about it. I know I am not alone or crazy. If you know what I am referring to, neither are you.

5. Finally, and most importantly, I had a comprehensive axillary node dissection. So, in addition to no IVs, blood draws or blood pressure cuffs on that left side

FOR LIFE, I was explicitly prohibited from any future laser hair removal anywhere on the left arm, which also includes the armpit. This restriction relates to the perpetual concern of triggering infection and the subsequent lymphedema. With the possibility of permanent bilateral armpit smoothness gone forever, my only remaining option was to have a right-side-only laser job. This solved only half of my problem and didn't seem worth the effort.

What was I to do with these depilation challenges? I didn't have a time machine, so the radio commercial suggestion of Ideal Image was no longer an option. I also didn't want to be constantly self-conscious about sleeveless summer dresses either. After appropriate research and trial and error, I finally found my solution: Gillette Venus Swirl razors with their unique Flexiball technology that contours to the curves of the body. They're damn expensive, but I went to Sam's Club and bought those cartridges in bulk. Then I signed up for Sirius XM.

The House that Cancer Built

As I alluded to earlier, the novelty of doing nothing productive during my convalescence wore off quickly. When I wasn't feeling crummy, I was bored. I tried to keep myself busy rearranging the furniture and reorganizing the bookshelves and kids' toys during my short spurts of usable energy. It wasn't enough. I needed something bigger, more purposeful. I needed a dream. I needed to finally build my house.

Just a little background. Three years prior, we "temporarily" moved into the small yellow rental house on South Lexington Avenue in White Plains, NY. We were really looking for a piece of land to buy. Our realtor laughed loudly at us,

"There's no empty land here. It's Westchester. This area has been overbuilt for more than 50 years."

Clearly, the woman had never met my mother, the heroine saint of all impossible tasks. With the gauntlet thrown down firmly at her feet, my mother got to work. She set off to the Housing Department with a map of the area printed out by my father and befriended a woman named Mary. Delving through all the non-electronic old town records together, my mother and Mary identified a list of six potential buildable lots. Slight problem: none of them were currently for sale. That didn't stop my Mother, not by a long shot. We devised a plan. She and I approached the various owners by different methods, including going door-to-door and cold calling them with phone numbers I found on reverse 411 (you enter the address and get back the phone number). One bright autumn day, we knocked on the door of a beautiful Victorian home that belonged to an 89-year-old woman named Beatrice Pfiester. We cheerily presented our proposal to purchase a side lot adjoining her gracious home. She immediately slammed the door in our faces while proclaiming,

"Not over my dead body."

Two years later, Beatrice Pfiester died of natural causes. Her stately Victorian with its sprawling property went on the open market. I pounced immediately, contacting the broker and offering to purchase the land separately from the house. He said he'd talk to the owners, who in turn said they needed to think about it. Apparently, Beatrice had 10 children, all of whom had to decide together. Collectively, they said, "No." They were concerned that if they sold off the piece of land, they would not be able to sell the main house. When I thought all hope was lost, Betty the superhero, a lawyer, and realtor, swooped in to save the day. She had an idea that was so far-fetched, it just might work. She and my brother Zvi would buy the house and flip it. We would buy the adjacent land, gaining the opportunity to build our dream home.

"Do you even have that kind of money?"

"Not yet, but we'll find it."

Betty was a believer. Now in her mid-40s, she had survived lymphoma in her 20s, later to suffer the death of both her parents in close succession. She re-approached the family with our new offer. For weeks, we heard nothing. It was another agonizing wait. Finally, the Pfiester family accepted. Three months later, I found myself sitting at the closing table in the offices of the Sutton Title Company, signing a contract for the purchase of a 0.39-acre piece of empty land.

Then I got cancer!

Our rental house was 100-years-old with a leaky roof. This meant that buckets full of rain streamed into the children's playroom every time there was a storm. All the windows in the house were single pane and un-insulated. The cold air blasted through during the chilly winter months. We had to jack the thermostat up to eighty degrees just to keep the overall ambient temperature livable. Our monthly utility bills were exorbitant. More annoying, as I've mentioned, the second-floor bathroom was shared between me, the two girls (Milla was still in diapers) and Alex. The shower was a tub with a plastic curtain that had been ripped off repeatedly by the force of my children demanding to see me "Maked" (Scarlett's word for naked).

All of this was manageable, even charming...when I was well. The kids were in that bathroom constantly tag-team peeing or playing in the sink. We had learned to be patient when I wanted to insert a tampon or Alex needed to take a dump. But when the Adriamycin hit my system and the nausea washed over me, I longed for the privacy of my own bathroom. I fantasized about a master bedroom with an en-suite bathroom, glass-encased shower and separate lockable door for the toilet. This was my chance, the only time in my frenetic life in which I could devote myself entirely to just one task. Cancer had slowed me down to a snail's pace and shaken me to my core. I needed to rebuild. I decided to make my dream a reality.

The first step before building a home is developing a site

plan, an outline of the building envelope that includes the property lines and setbacks. Then, the site plan needs approval from the town. This can be a very frustrating process. The approval gets bogged down in invisible layers of bureaucracy. Our paperwork got buried in a pile on the desk of a woman named Sue Murphy. Sue was an associate in the Engineering Department and a strict nine-to-fiver. I had called her office several times but was always told the same three things, *"Sue is in a meeting," "Sue is at lunch"* or *"Sue just stepped away from her desk." "I can send you to her voicemail,"* the secretary would offer with annoyance for the millionth time.

I was stuck. To start building our home, I needed a greenlight on the site plan. But to get this done, I first needed Sue to return my calls. I grew desperate. It was time to play the cancer card again.

On Friday, December 20th, I crashed her Christmas party. The entire personnel of the Department of Public Works were crammed into their office on the second floor of City Hall. There were sandwiches, pizza, and alcoholic and non-alcoholic drinks. Most importantly, Sue Murphy was in there somewhere. I arrived sans makeup with my head covering intentionally riding high to reveal that I was bald underneath. It was clear that I was undergoing chemotherapy. Upon my pitiable request, Sue Murphy emerged from the crowd. She was a tiny woman, not at all what I had pictured given the power she yielded over me. Embarrassed and apologetic, she immediately ran to her desk to retrieve some papers. She returned, sat down next to me, and skimmed the plans for two minutes. They had already been reviewed and signed by another junior engineer. Astonishingly, she signed them. Now we could begin.

We had decided to build the house modularly, which meant that it would be assembled in a factory in Pennsylvania, then transported in five modules to Westchester. The purpose was to cut down on cost and speed up the timeline. We hired a builder from New Jersey named Bob Mazola. Bob was a good guy. He was much more accessible than any other contractor I've ever encountered. We spent numerous hours over the phone clarifying the specifications for the house. All the data was stored in an excel file on my laptop that I accessed from my bedroom. On my worst weak days, my mom would drive to Bob's office in Montvale, NJ. The three of us would conference call while I sat propped up in my bed in White Plains and they sat together with tracing paper, revising the plans.

Every two weeks, my mom would accompany me to my treatments and we would spread out the large house plans on my lap as they probed my damaged veins for IV access. The nurses in the chemo suite at Phelps Memorial Hospital referred to me as "the girl with the blueprints." Once the Benadryl kicked in, though, I would lose my focus.

The tasks before me were formidable: applying for a jumbo mortgage, designing a house without an architect and making hundreds of major and minor decisions. Whenever I got derailed, my mom would get me back on track.

"Keep your eyes on the prize Tali. You can do this."

My mother had the visual-spatial perception of an architect without any formal training. I had spent my childhood in the two-story house she had designed for our family. Now at night, instead of nightmares, I began to dream of a steam shower with large gray tiles on the walls. I yearned for a cozy office off the bedroom where I could take hospital calls and look at radiologic imaging for consults without waking Alex up 20 times a night. During the day, the countless nitty-gritty details of choosing door knobs and faucet handles distracted me from feeling useless and unemployed. And then, one magical day, the final drawings were approved and the construction, albeit in the far-away Simplex factory, began.

The day they began to dig out the foundation, I was buzzing with excitement. The yellow CAT digger trucks rolled onto our property and began hungrily clawing into the earth. Piles of rocks and dirt were strewn to the sides, leaving behind a monstrous hole. Soon, the excavators filled the void with metal and concrete and set the foundation for our home.

Blessedly, my father was still able to stand on his own when the modules were delivered on enormous wide-load trucks. These pieces were masterfully assembled by cranes. I framed a picture of him, proud and smiling with the building blocks of our home laid out in the backdrop. I prayed that he would see the project to its completion, but that was not meant to be.

Our new house saved my life that year. The process of its creation had given me purpose and the drive to get up every morning. It was the house that cancer built, but God, it was the most beautiful one I could ever imagine.

The Funeral

*"When the patriarch Jacob believed his son
Joseph was dead, he tore his garments."*
                                        -Genesis 37:34

My father died exactly one week before we moved into our
newly constructed house, never stepping foot in the first-floor
bedroom that I'd designed for him. It was a Friday night and
he took his last breaths peacefully, in his own home. He was
never alone. He was loved well until the moment he died, surrounded by family. In the hours before his death, my mother
and brothers alternated sitting around his rented hospital bed
in the living room. While we all sensed it was coming, I could
not be there that weekend, because I was on-call. Immediately
after the Sabbath ended, my cell phone rang. It was Betty calling and I instantly knew why.

"I'm so sorry, Tali. Your father passed away."

I spent the next thirty minutes frantically texting and
phoning my various partners in search of immediate coverage
for the hospital. Only once that was secured did I sit down to
write his eulogy.

The words and thoughts had been swirling around in my

head for months, uncongealed and nebulous. Now it was time to put them down on paper. I started...*"I have always been a Daddy's girl. I'm not ashamed to admit it. But, when you have a father such as mine, it is an honor that I am proud of, not at all a hindrance..."*

At his funeral, the next day, there were approximately one thousand people. It was standing room only. Nevertheless, the cavernous room of the sanctuary was absolutely silent. Afterwards, there was a short procession to the hearse outside. We drove immediately to JFK airport. As per his wishes, we planned to bury him in Jerusalem, Israel. It was the country where he was raised, where his parents lived and died and where his two brothers resided.

My brothers, Zvi, Dov and J.J., my mother and I arrived at the airport together. We had already performed the act of kriah. Kriah is a Hebrew word meaning "tearing." It refers to the act of tearing one's clothes. This rending is an old tradition that is mentioned throughout the Bible as an expression of grief and anger at the loss of a loved one. The act of tearing is performed by the children, parents, spouse, and siblings of the deceased. Kriah is always performed standing. The act of standing shows strength at a time of grief. A cut is made on the left side of the clothing for parents, over the heart, and on the right side for all other relatives. Weaving through the airport with only small carry-ons, we formed an obvious unit of a grieving family, eyes puffy, dark clothes torn.

We boarded the plane knowing that my father's body was in the cargo hold. I sat next to Dov for the eleven-hour flight to Tel Aviv. Most of my interactions with him during that time in my life were in the setting of family gatherings. There was typically a lot of bustling, children running around, and cousins tickling and chasing each other. But, during my father's several admissions to the hospital, we had some quiet adult time. Mostly, we'd sit at a small table in the kosher family eating room of the Milstein Pavilion. We would discuss our father's health, potential clinical trials, his homecare, next steps, etc. There was scant time for feelings or personal grievances. Even if there had been, my family wasn't great at that form of communication.

Throughout our lives, my family often spent vacations, holidays and weekends together. Once they were married and had children, two of my three brothers moved back to the same town that my parents lived in. As siblings, we talked a lot at the dinner table, covering a wide variety of topics in such an animated fashion that it was always difficult to be heard. But, ever since we were kids, we shied away from confrontation, especially with each other. Betty always said that the difference between us and her family was that her family members were very upfront with each other. If any of her seven siblings did wrong, they were immediately rebuked by least one other sibling. In contrast, it took me almost a year to start the conversation I was about to have with my brother on that darkened airplane.

I shifted in my seat awkwardly, building the courage to speak.

"I need to tell you something. It's something that I've been holding on to for months, pretty much since last summer."

"What is it?"

He was about to swallow an Ambien so that he could sleep through the flight. Our schedule after landing was tight and stressful and we all needed the rest.

"You can take it and I'll explain before it kicks in. Then, you can fall asleep and forget everything I said."

I began to explain.

"I had an expectation, maybe unfairly so, that the minute I revealed my own cancer diagnosis, my siblings would rally around me and champion me the whole way through. Instead, I felt abandoned. You were all there when I woke up from my first surgery. I thought I am lucky. My three brothers are really supporting me. But that was it. In all those hard months of chemo, you rarely drove the hour to White Plains to make sure that I was ok. You only saw me when I drove to New Jersey to see Aba."

He looked ashamed, embarrassed, but also really surprised.

"I thought you were fine. You always seemed ok. I thought you had it all under control. I didn't realize..."

I knew he was right. My brothers had seen me on my upswings, the midway points between treatments, when I was coming up for air and before I got shoved back under the water again. In the interim, I communicated with my sisters-in-law, who they viewed as their proxies. Maybe I didn't clearly express my need. Maybe I projected too good an image. Maybe I sounded too alert on the phone during our numerous conference calls about my father when, really I lay groggy in bed.

"I know. I needed you to figure it out anyway... Mom was totally overwhelmed. I got that. Most of her energy went into caring for Aba. I know you did a crazy amount for him, too. You and Zvi were the ones living nearby, always over there helping and responding to emergencies. You dealt with many crises. You have such busy lives and I have always been so preoccupied with my medical career. So, I felt guilty asking for help. I wasn't sure I deserved it."

"What could I have done?"

"Shown up on a Sunday and taken the girls to the park or to the zoo. My friends offered, but the kids were always too scared. They wouldn't go anywhere away from me. Juliette would wrap herself like a cobra around the railing whenever we tried to send her out on a playdate. With family though, I think it would have been different. Alex and I struggled to made it work and we did. But it was tough, really really tough."

"I'm sorry. I should have known better. I didn't know."

"Thank you. That helps. You can sleep now. It's ok."

I, too, drifted off. Some of the crushing burden of disappointment had been lifted, though it was not completely gone.

In the morning, when we landed, we drove straight to Jerusalem. We buried my father on the western edge of the city, in a cemetery known as Har Hamenuchot, the "Mount of Those Who Are Resting." He had a corner plot with expansive views of the tree-dotted hills of Judea. In that same burial ground lay the remains of his parents, grandparents and numerous aunts, uncles and extended family. As is customary for Jews in Israel, his body was laid to rest directly in the ground, in a simple shroud, without a coffin.

We split the seven-day mourning period of Shiva. The first few days were spent at my uncle's house in Israel and the last days in the United States. Distant relatives, family and personal friends poured in from every part of my father's past. They regaled us with countless stories, detailing how he had impacted their lives. When we flew back home, we left a piece of ourselves buried in the ancient city with my father, never to be replaced. Back in New Jersey, we sat Shiva in the family room of my brother Zvi's house. Members of the community, more relatives, friends and business colleagues waited on long lines to pay their respects. They, too, had stories to tell.

Returning to my newly built house in White Plains after Shiva, I had the unsettling feeling of being an intruder. I laid in Juliette's bed staring at her six-over-one double-paned windows, charming chandelier and my-favorite-color-of-lavender walls, crying by the glow of her nightlight. I lost my father, the most important figure in my life, at the very same time my future was coming back into focus.

What About the Husband?

In these situations, husbands tend to be either martyred or marginalized. My ever-patient spouse was no exception. Polite people remembered to ask, *"How is Alex holding up?"* or *"How has he been dealing with all this?"* Typically, I answered, *"Fine, I guess"* or *"Pretty good, I think."*

"But how is he really?"

It was a tough call. He seemed fine. He woke up every day, showered and got dressed, just like before. He scooped up Scarlett and hugged Juliette with the same fatherly zest as before. For months, he kissed me on my patchy, bald head as he left for work each morning while I lay there languid, and generally not as before. This wasn't the wife he signed up for.

For as long as he'd known me, I had worked my way through sinus infections, exhaustion and morning sickness x3 pregnancies with unwavering determination. I had dressed in the pre-dawn darkness, showered and ran out the door before he rolled over to feel the empty spot beside him. I drove our Subaru, in the dead of winter, over mounds of unpaved snow to fearlessly race to the Children's Hospital of Philadelphia for airway emergencies. During the years of my training, I began my productive day while he still slept softly in our bed. I was a rock; then, I became a wet rag. In place of the empty spot, there was now a deep impression in the mattress of a woman who had barely left the bed since the summer. How should he be?

In the immediate aftermath of my diagnosis, Alex was disturbingly calm. His knee-jerk response to my need for a mastectomy may seem offensive. For me, it was a testament to his resilience.

"Let's Angelina-Jolie those suckers off ASAP, ok Babes? I don't care. I just want you better."

We never cried, at least, not together. Of course, I cried a lot on my own. We never mourned the loss of my health, my body or our faith in a long future together. We simply adjusted to our new reality without discussing it. Just like when Milla was born. We had a child who lived in the intensive care unit of the hospital for several months. It became routine: wake up, go to the NICU/ see our baby, go to work, go to the NICU/ see our baby, come home/see our other children and so on. So, too, with this. A routine was born as outlined by my shifting treatment schedules. We followed along, hoping we'd end up on the other side of this hell.

I realized later that during the darkest times, I really didn't know what Alex was feeling. I was so desperate for his support and crushed by my own vulnerability that I left him alone to deal with his pain. It took a silent toll. Regarding the medical details, I often excluded him. I was trying to protect him, but in the process, I inadvertently sidelined him instead. It's amazing how much you can weather in a relationship without understanding what your spouse or significant other is experiencing. Despite our best intentions, we both battled some of our demons alone.

Sometimes we joked that Alex is the man behind the woman behind the man. It alluded to the equality between us as a couple and our lack of traditional 'wifely' or 'husbandly' roles. We just believed in making it work. For example, he cooked because he's great at it and he enjoyed it more. I did the girls' hair because I can braid and make a relatively straight part. Similarly, I dressed them because I can match tutu skirts with pink sequined tops. Also, I covered all trips to the pediatrician and dentist because I know the right questions to ask. He did all sports activities with them, including ice-skating and swimming, because he is athletic, and I am not.

For the six weeks post-mastectomy that I was prohibited from lifting Milla, he handled all middle of the night wake ups and feeds. When I became stronger, we switched back and I did. Later, during my "on" weeks of chemo, he woke up with her again. Then, on my "off" weeks, it was me once more. Throughout the long months, we continued the silent game of "who is closer to breaking?" Whoever lost got to take over bath time, bedtime and early weekend breakfasts. For a long while, it was usually him. During that period, I took it for granted that Alex was always ok. I convinced myself that because he never showed his fear, he probably wasn't afraid. More likely, that was just what I wanted to believe.

Every year, on Thanksgiving Day, Alex's family gathers together at his parents' house in Cherry Hill, New Jersey. All his aunts, cousins and their children come for an elaborate meal and then hang out chatting late into the night. That year, Thanksgiving occurred in the middle-end of chemo. I was sitting on my in-law's couch, dressed up for the holiday. My bare head was covered while I chatted with Alex's first cousin, Olga.

She asked how we were doing. I mentioned innocently how well Alex has been handling everything.

"It's strange though, you know, he's never really broken down and cried."

"Well, just not in front of you. Right?"

She looked at me as if she had just said something so obvious. I felt utterly stupid.

I had always attributed Alex's stoicism to his military training. In the aftermath of 9/11, Alex, a proud American but an immigrant by birth, had joined the Army Reserves, specifically the Military Intelligence division. What I gathered from his recounting of that time is that many of the drills are unbearably tough. His buddy Chris Green, a red-haired, blue-eyed Mormon from Salt Lake City, told me that during basic training, they dubbed him, "The Horse." According to him, Alex would lug his rucksack through 20-mile hikes in the hot desert. Despite being exhausted, he never complained. He encouraged others while consistently leading the pack. I loved this fantastical image of Alex, a broad-built six-foot-two man with nostrils flaring, drenched in sweat in the Arizona desert, so handsome in his fatigues. Beyond the military lore, I had seen this same rugged determination with my own eyes several times in the last few years. More recently, he had dragged me and our family with an invisible rope through the frictional sand, always encouraging me,

"You can do it, Babes. Buck up."

"I don't want to go to chemo today."

*"I know Babycakes. I know it's hard. You **have** to."*

During the traffic-filled four-hour drive back home from South Jersey, I finally asked Alex if he thought at some point we should *really* talk about it.

"It, what?"

"It, it."

"Could you be more specific?"

"You know."

"Not entirely. Still not getting you."

"Like, the cancer I could die thing, 'it.'"

"Oh, that thing. Nope. Why, do you?"

"I don't think so. What's the point?"

"Let's just keep getting through it. You feel me tiny-strong-hands?"

"I feel you."

Alex's favorite nickname for me, "tiny, strong hands" is a nod to my abilities as a surgeon masked in my small, size 6 gloves, feminine hands.

Truth is, every couple gets to choose how they manage their curveballs. There is no perfect way, just a way that works for you as a team. For us, Alex was all about charging onward, past the crappy part and on to the next part where I was healthy again. His positive outlook was my buoy in the shit storm and I clung to it for strength and hope. Sometimes, his comments may have been crass, but he made me smile when I really needed it.

Later, in the midst of radiation treatments, Alex and I sat in the kitchen, after the kids were finally asleep. We were discussing another woman in our community who had very recently undergone a bilateral mastectomy. She also had young children, although not babies and toddlers like ours. Since she had the newer diagnosis, the communal helping/cooking machine was now revving up for her. Alex and I had spent so much time in the limelight that we were ready to step back into the crowd for a while.

"I guess we're losing our celebrity status. Now, I will become an ordinary girl who had cancer," I commented sarcastically.

He, in turn, became very serious and looked at me intensely.

"You will never be ordinary. You will always be special. You are not just some woman who lost her tatas. You are a sophisticated, smart young woman doctor and your story will always be interesting."

It was a really touching moment to hear him talk about me like that, especially given how hard I'd been on him those past months. I looked at him lovingly. Wait … did he just say "tatas?" What am I, a topless dancer? It was so ridiculously inappropriate that my reaction was extreme; tears were cascading down my face. In that moment, for the first time I could remember since this whole mess began, they were tears of laughter.

Rotten Eggs

With three kids and three adults in our household, we go through a lot of eggs. Still, I have yet to figure out how long I can leave raw eggs in the refrigerator before they go bad. Unlike milk, they don't give off a telltale smell when they are spoiled. And if they have been sitting around a long time, is it better to take them out and cook them? Would they keep longer that way?

I once asked my mother this question and she answered that you can test the egg by dunking it in a cup of cold water. If it sinks, it's good; if it floats, throw it out. But, when should I start checking? I mean, how long are they *supposed* to last? The farm fresh cage-free hormone-free eggs we now buy are devoured so quickly, I rarely worry about it. Lately, I've been wondering about my own eggs. How long until their expiration date? Have they gone bad already?

In my mind, I was going to have four children. After all, I come from a family of four, my two older brothers both had four children, albeit one from a blended family. My youngest brother had three children under the age of five, but I suspected was planning on expansion. Four always felt like my magical number, the amount of kids it took to form a real brood. Growing up, there was always one sibling to fight with, one to band together with against the first and a spare in case one was away at camp or sick. The plan was to pull a reversal of my original family structure. Instead of three boys and a girl, I'd have three daughters and a son. I was three-quarters of the way there.

I had been achieving my goal rapidly, starting with Juliette's birth roughly ten months after our wedding. Less than two years after Juliette was born, feisty Scarlett joined our crew. In the delivery room, immediately after she pushed her way into the world, I turned to Alex and declared,

"Don't get too comfortable, we're having a third."

Twenty-three months later, at about the size of a small roaster chicken, Milla made her early arrival into our lives. Her birth was so terrifying that I didn't say a word afterward. When she finally graduated from the NICU and began growing, my heart began to yearn for that bonus fourth child. Very soon after that, before I could get cracking on my agenda, I was thrust into a very different reality. *Cancer.* Would I even be around for the three children I already had?

Initially, as I listened to the litany of required treatment modalities, I was much less phased by a decade of Tamoxifen maintenance therapy than I was by having my boobs chopped off or missing tons of work. But, as I began to digest the information, I realized that the chance to complete my ideal family was slipping away from me. Chemotherapy would induce a menopause-like state. Then, even if this process eventually reversed itself and my ovaries recovered, the anti-estrogen medication I'd be prescribed would be teratogenic (likely to cause defect or death) to any developing fetus I could conceive.

I called my fertility doctor, Dr. Klein, to discuss my options. He explained that I had a very small window, right after my oncologic surgery and before starting chemotherapy, in which he could stimulate my ovaries and retrieve my eggs. These eggs could be frozen or fertilized with my husband's sperm and then stored. To what end? While on the Tamoxifen, I couldn't become pregnant anyway and that was a ten-year stretch. In a decade, I'd be 46 turning 47 and getting pregnant at that point sounded absurd. Alternatively, and much more expensively, I could use a surrogate. It seemed insane to go through that costly and difficult process. What if I wound up with a nutty sink-peeing-blond-lady like Amy Poehler in "Baby Mama" carrying my baby? Not to mention what the egg retrieval process would entail. It would have been a different story if I had no children.

While I agonized over this decision, the game changed anyway. Once my pathology came back with widespread lymph node metastases, Dr. Klein wouldn't touch me with a ten-foot pole. No respectable fertility specialist would inject a hormone receptor positive breast cancer patient with stimulating hormones. The door to my fantasy family had slammed firmly in my face. During those first months, the image of our tightly packed minivan faded into the background. I needed to address a more pressing issue: the advanced nature of my disease. Procreative concerns took a back seat to my desire to stay alive.

Time passes, though, and we forget. When the seasons of fighting my illness slowly gave way to the long years of keeping cancer at bay, the nagging sense of loss resurfaced. Not the loss of a child, exactly, but the loss of my choice to have another. Most days, I barely kept afloat between work and patients and kids and sleep deprivation. People would think I was nuts for even considering adding to the chaos that is my life. Nevertheless, it was hard waking up each morning and swallowing a 20-mg pill that damned my choices... even though it kept my boogeyman away.

I was not foolish enough to poke the sleeping lion of my cancer. I wouldn't because I had too much to lose if it woke up and decided to bite my head off. I tried not to dwell on my ovaries or think about rotting eggs. I tried to stop picturing Alex playing hockey in the street behind our house with our imaginary son. I strived every day to remember that I was lucky because my life was full enough and because I knew that my lovely family was someone else's fantasy. And on days I lost perspective, Milla's 1 and 3 AM wakeups, with blood curdling screams, with hair covered in pee and snot, were there to remind me.

And if those powerful reminders ever ceased, there was always adoption.

Giant Pink Tents

My first attempt at an official breast cancer walk was the "Making Strides Walk of Westchester." It was nearly a bust. In between Alex's 7 am soccer game and Scarlett's afternoon tennis lesson, I hastily changed into a pink sweatshirt and leggings. I was already armed with a streak of "cotton candy" colored hair that I had dyed for October's breast cancer awareness month. I applied a double layer of bright pink lipstick to complete the effect. It was one year from the date of my initial diagnosis. With Juliette dressed to match and buckled in the backseat, I pulled out of the driveway, already 40 minutes behind the suggested arrival time. The walk began at 9:30 on a frigidly cold autumn morning. At 9:15, my GPS lied and promised I was a mere 10 minutes away. It was tight. Hopefully, I was going to make it. I pulled off Route 684 and saw the sign for Manhattanville College when my GPS chimed,

"Turn right in 500 feet then your destination is on the left."

9:25, almost there, we are golden. Oh crap! I saw the flashing lights of the police car and the "No Turn" barricade across the exit to the right. The two officers were motioning all the cars to the left, back onto the highway. Fine, no problem. The British woman's voice kindly redirected me. In truth, there was a problem. Every single approach to the event was blocked with apologetic cops.

"Are we lost, Mommy? Can't we just ask Siri for help?"

"I don't think Siri knows about the police blockades."

She didn't believe me.

I tried to use the time as we drove around in circles to explain to Juliette, now six-and-one-quarter, the purpose of the walk. Should I use the words "breast cancer?" I didn't want to spook her. I did want to seize this opportunity to teach her about perseverance and strength. I chose my words carefully.

"Remember when Mommy was sick?"

I saw her nod in the rearview mirror, distracted by *Frozen* playing for the zillionth time on the screen in front of her.

"Today is a day for helping other people who are sick to get better."

"But, you're not sick."

"Not now. I was. Do you remember?"

*"Yes, that was a **long** time ago."*

Not for me, I thought to myself.

After four failed attempts at entry and additional consultation with Waze, I finally found a way in. I parked in a back lot marked "Silver and Gold." Juliette and I hopped a ride on a golf-cart shuttling people to the starting line. With cold wind blowing on our faces, we were warmed by the tightly packed women sitting beside us. When we disembarked, Juliette's brown eyes widened with glee.

*"Mommy, you didn't tell me it was going to be a **PINK** carnival!"*

She jumped with joy and we headed towards the crowd. We purchased two adorable matching pink ski hats with the

"American Cancer Society" logo. We snapped several selfies in front of the "MAKE YOUR STRIDE COUNT" display of hundreds of multi-shaded pink ribbons. I immediately posted the pictures, mostly because my skin looked great in the sunlight that day. We must have made a good-looking mother-daughter pair because we caught the eye of a photographer covering the event. He asked if we had time for a photo shoot and offered to email me the pictures. By the time we were done, it was 10 am and the walk had already begun. Juliette was drinking complementary hot chocolate, likely intended for the people who completed the 2.5-mile course. The nice women manning the refreshments didn't judge.

We continued to explore the various tents, filled with pink pens, raffle tickets and merchandise raising money for cancer research. In the distance, I spotted a giant pink tent marked "Survivors." I approached it tentatively, with Juliette hopping alongside me, her metallic pink ribbon necklace bouncing on her chest. Did I really belong in there? A 90-year-old volunteer eagerly greeted me at the doorway.

"Are you a survivor?"

Unexpectedly, I felt myself choking on the answer.

"Yes, I am."

"How many years?" she probed.

"Since my diagnosis or completing treatment?"

"Either one."

"One full year, I guess."

She scribbled on her paper then smiled at me encouragingly.

"Well dear, that's a start."

Minutes later, I exited the tent with my Survivor sticker applied prominently above my left reconstructed breast.

I AM A

1

YEAR SURVIVOR

I used to feel cancer was a very solitary experience. The first weeks after my diagnosis, I walked around like I was harboring a dirty little secret. It was too deeply personal for me to share with others. At that point, I had only discussed the awful news with my husband, my parents and three siblings and a handful of close friends. It felt like the first trimester of pregnancy. Eventually, your secret becomes more challenging to hide as it robs you of your strength, your hair and your spirit. Cancer and its cure become an un-concealable nine-month belly.

That day, surrounded by throngs of families and women dressed in all sorts of audacious pink accessories, tutus and face paint, I finally accepted an undeniable truth: I am not alone in my journey, not by a long-shot. And it's a good thing, because there is power in numbers. I let this realization wash over me as Juliette and I walked past the bandstand. Taylor Swift's verses echoed in the air.

But I keep cruising, can't stop, won't stop moving ...like I got this music in my mind saying it's gonna be alright.

Juliette was dancing, swerving in step with the beat, covered from head to toe in pink. She was beaming, her new adult teeth peeking through her top gums crookedly, a sure sign that in the next five years, she'd need braces. I couldn't help believing...Yeah, maybe it will be.

The Machine

Even as a multi-year survivor, breast cancer complications continue threatening to pop up at every turn. Previously, I mentioned the feared complication: lymphedema. When axillary lymph nodes are removed during breast surgery with sentinel node biopsy or axillary dissection or are treated with radiation therapy, some of the lymph vessels can become blocked. This may prevent lymph fluid from leaving the area. Lymphedema occurs when lymph fluid collects in the arm or other areas such as the hands, fingers, chest or back, causing that area to swell (edema). The swelling may be so slight it's barely seen or felt. Or, it may be so great that the arm grows very large. In severe cases, lymphedema can cause pain and limit movement. Also, it can be quite upsetting to have one arm become larger than the other, even if the difference is small.

One of the biggest problems with lymphedema is that it's unpredictable. It typically surfaces within the first three years after surgery, although sometimes it's more immediate. There are no warning signs. Some of the risk factors include having a large number of axillary lymph nodes removed, like me, or having axillary lymph nodes removed AND radiation therapy, like me, again. Other factors include having a large number of axillary lymph nodes that contain cancer, damn, "yes" to that, too, and being overweight, finally, a "no." Even before there is visible swelling, there is often a sensory change such as the feeling of heaviness, tightness or tingling. This can come and go.

The problem is that once lymphedema develops, it can only be controlled or minimized. It never resolves completely. It's an isolating emotion to be afraid of something that most people have never even heard of and can barely understand. It occurs so arbitrarily that I felt like I was playing duck, duck goose with all the other breast cancer survivors. I was stuck sitting in this vulnerable circle, hoping not to be "it."

"Your left arm looks doughy."

Julie, my physical therapist, looked more concerned than usual.

"It does. Where?"

"Right here below the elbow. It wasn't the last time you were here, I'm sure of it. Did you notice?"

"Well, I wasn't sure, maybe."

I had noticed something, a few months back after flying to Las Vegas for a medical conference, right after getting fitted for my compression sleeve and discovering my 'imperfect' anatomy. When I landed, I looked down and thought my left arm was slightly bigger than my right, even under the sleeve. It felt slightly heavier, too. I kept staring at it. The difference was subtle enough that I really couldn't tell. I had been so nervous about developing lymphedema all this time that I couldn't distinguish between my anxiety and reality. It was too awkward to ask the passenger next to me,

"Excuse me, sir, sorry to bother you, do my arms look different sizes to you?"

Here, however, was someone who was trained in this arena. So, I asked,

"What do I do now?"

"The most important thing is to get it under control. We don't want it to get any worse."

Julie began manual lymphatic drainage (MLD) which is a massage of the affected area to manually move lymph fluid from the swollen region into the lymph nodes that are still functioning. The fluid can then be transported away through the circulatory system. Julie outlined a few conceivable options, including wearing that hated compression sleeve all day every day and a technique called "compression wrapping." Both were incompatible with scrubbing in for surgery.

"You might be a good candidate for the compression machine, assuming we can get your insurance to pay for it. It costs several thousand dollars, but Cassandra, the rep, has been very helpful in making it go through for some of my other patients."

Amazingly, my insurance did approve the device without much of a fight. I guess it's hard to argue against the necessity of a working surgeon having all upper limbs functional. I couldn't possibly walk around for weeks with my arm bandaged up to the shoulder. Soon, a giant box arrived via FedEx. A man called me from the company to set up a time to meet at my house for a demonstration. To my surprise, for once, the available appointments were late at night and allowed me to finish my regular day.

Rick, the nurse, showed up at 7:30 pm that Wednesday. He

was much hotter and more muscular than I'd expected. He was also very nice. We needed a space where we could talk privately for him to program my settings and to instruct me how to use the device. Upon my suggestion, we snuck up to my bedroom while the girls were occupied eating dinner. Just like Rick, the Tactile Flexitouch™ full arm and core pneumatic compression device is a sight to behold. It's a giant one-piece brown fabric suit with long sleeves and shorts. It has various air chambers that inflate and deflate sequentially, creating a wave-like motion that directs lymph fluid away from the impaired area of the limb (axilla) towards functioning regions such as the groin. In the groin, the lymph fluid can be absorbed by the body and processed. Getting into this contraption is complicated and must be performed carefully. The multiple Velcro straps must be fastened in a very precise manner and order.

While Rick was leaning over me and tightening the Velcro, Scarlett burst in the room.

"What is this man doing, Mommy?"

"He's showing me how to use this massage machine."

"Why do you need a massage?"

"You know, sweetie, to relax me."

"What's the man's name?"

"Rick... Say hi to Rick, Scarlie."

"Hi Rick. Why are you here to massage Mommy in her bed?"

I didn't look up to see if Rick's skin was as crimson as mine. I avoided eye contact throughout the remainder of his instructions. Later, I thought it wise to omit the details of Rick's physique when relaying this funny story to Alex. Eventually,

Scarlett became bored with all the technicalities and returned downstairs.

The Velcro quality of the straps is industrial strength. Rick warned me not to go near any nice sweaters or woven blankets or the two may never detach. Also, to prevent your body oils from getting on the fabric, you need to wear loosely fitted long-sleeved shirts underneath the suit. The issue with that is that it can get very hot being tightly bundled in an overlying layer of un-breathable heavy fabric. After getting completely strapped in, you need to shimmy your body onto the bed without disconnecting the hoses from the controller box. Once you've finally gotten into the proper position, you can't move too suddenly, or one of the four hoses will inevitably detach.

When Rick was there, he made it all seem so easy, but there's a reason the company made a YouTube video about it. After he left, I watched it several times. On the following night when I was on my own, things didn't go as smoothly. I remembered how to step into the shorts section, and even how to tighten the arm straps and chest wrap. I rolled onto my bed, pressed start and was on my way. As soon as it started inflating, I realized that I'd left the television controller on the dresser instead of the night stand. I had to unfasten and disrobe all over again. On the second night, I remembered the remote and forgot an extra pillow to elevate my arm. The result was the same. Many times, the box flipped over and fell to the ground. Retrieving it in this full-body armor was tricky business. Eventually, I got the hang of it. Now I needed to find the time to use it. My treatment program was scheduled to last an entire hour. Rick encouraged me to look at it like required leisure time.

"Just watch a movie or read a book and relax. It's like going to the spa."

Well, that sounds very appealing. Where is this nightly magical hour and why is it so damn hard to find? Clearly, the girls need to be fast asleep before I can commit to strapping myself into this apparatus. On the other hand, Alex did not want to be in the room while I was using it because it freaked him out. It was a bulky, crazy looking thing and in it, I looked like a thin Sumo wrestler. I found the hum of the cycling expansion and release of air soothing. It had the familiar sound of a ventilator in the intensive care unit. Understandably, Alex was not interested in associating that image with me.

For the few months that I kept up with my treatments, Alex remained downstairs in the family room until the cycle was done. By the time he'd come to bed, it was nearly midnight. Rick had made the process seem so effortless, so why was it such a struggle? My only guess is that most of his other customers are 30 or more years my senior, have adult children who are no longer living at home, and/or spouses who are so hard of hearing that they aren't bothered by the noise at all.

I will admit that the machine did work. It reduced the asymmetry, but only while I continued to use it consistently. For me, the nightly commitment was nearly impossible, especially since I always fall asleep putting the kids to bed. So, for now, I keep it in the corner of my bedroom as a reminder of my delinquency. I'm hoping it will scare the lymphedema spirits away. It certainly looks intimidating to me. It has been gathering dust, but I keep promising myself...tomorrow will be different.

Abdominal Binders and Sexy Lingerie

While we're on the topic of scary things in the bedroom...as much as I would like to tackle the subject of intimacy after cancer with the same raw honesty that I have tried to provide throughout the rest of my tale, I can't. I made a promise to Alex that the juicy details of this topic were not open to the public. It is the sole request he made regarding this book and for that reason, I feel obligated to honor it. I can, however, talk in generalities because the subject matter is too important to gloss over.

Navigating intimacy after this type of illness is treacherous, especially for the man. The path is filled with twisty turns and steep cliffs around blind corners. It's like traveling in a foreign country before GPS and all the maps are locked away, but no one has the key. In almost every direction is a trap. The hapless husband tries valiantly to do the right thing at the right time. Even a casual compliment, like "Honey, you look good today," can result in a colossal fall-out. Can't he just know when to stay close and not to touch? Can't he sense when to touch but not to expect too much? Shouldn't he recognize, after being rejected repeatedly, when it is time to try again? The answer is "No." Yet, even when I knew I was being unfair, I still needed Alex to figure a lot out on his own.

Early on, I was in too much despair about my body to talk with him honestly. It is difficult to desire sex when your physical femininity has rebelled against you. Lucky for me, his intuition guided us through some dark places when I didn't know what I wanted myself. The key for me was to take it slowly, like I get into a swimming pool, feet first, gradually acclimating my body part by part to the water. For others, it may be best to jump right back in. There's an initial shock as you hit the water. Then, it feels great against your skin. You just need to figure out which type of person you are.

There are women who opt for the TRAM flap (described previously) in which the breast is immediately reconstructed at the time of initial excision with a muscle flap from the abdomen. The recovery from this surgery is slower and more painful. The advantage is that it can get the bulk of the job done in one step. As discussed, I had chosen the more traditional expander-to-implant route. As a result, my path to final reconstruction was longer, with a few unexpected detours that I would have gladly avoided. For example, I had an extra trip under the knife to remove an ellipse of non-healing skin near the excised left nipple before I could begin radiation. More recently, I needed to fill a certain hollow that my surgeon was still blaming on my naturally asymmetric chest wall. I am still not convinced. To fill this defect, fat needed to be harvested from somewhere else, basically translating into a free pass to get liposuction. Sounds awesome, right? That's what I thought.

I had finally found the upside in all this mess. I figured that I'd combine the liposuction with the nipple reconstruction and kill two birds with one stone.

My surgery was scheduled for a Thursday. I blocked off my office hours for Thursday and Friday and requested not to be on call that weekend, so I'd have additional time to recuperate. I should have talked to someone in more detail about the standard length of recovery. On Tuesday morning, the week of the surgery, I was at Maimonides for pre-op testing, more blood work, CXRs etc. I also had to meet with Pam, Dr. Gayle's physician's assistant for a quick review of the surgical plan and to get my prescriptions. She instructed me to come to surgery with a few choices of super tight full-body Spanx. I was in a rush to get back to my office, and I mentioned in passing that I planned to return to work on Monday and to the operating room on Tuesday morning after my surgery. She peered at me dubiously through her giant red-rimmed glasses.

"I don't think so. Noooo. You'll be in way too much pain from the skin grafts."

I had been really looking forward to waking up this time with all my anatomical parts back in place. No such luck. Dr. Gayle came in and affirmed her concerns.

"Even with the liposuction alone, you may still be pretty uncomfortable..." He hesitated, *"I guess you'll be ok for work on Monday."*

I was not encouraged, but it was too late. As usual, my patient schedule was loaded up with surgeries and packed office hours for the upcoming week, to make up for the two days I was already missing.

"The nipple reconstruction will definitely have to be saved for a later date."

Yay! Another surgery. Just what I need.

Little did I know then that the later date would never come...

By now, Alex and I had become accustomed to the routine of waking up in the dark at about 4:30 am, leaving the house by 5 and beginning the search for parking in Brooklyn by 6. I always asked to be the first surgical case of the day and they usually granted my request. When I arrived in the pre-op area that morning, Dr. Gayle began again with the elaborate planning drawings on my body. He was nice enough to say that he wasn't sure where he'd find any fat because I was so skinny. I gladly pointed out my "problem areas." I drifted off to anesthetic sleep calmly this time with the knowledge that Dr. Gayle was finally removing something that I wanted to lose. When I woke up from anesthesia, my chest was again mummified in this sticky foam-like substance and my abdomen was wrapped up tight.

When we got home, I crawled into my bed, pleasantly surprised by the lack of pain. Over the whole weekend, I took it very easy. My mom stayed at our house and helped with the kids and I slept most of the day on Saturday. By Sunday evening, it dawned on me that I was supposed to be at full capacity for work the next morning and I started to freak out. The binder was really confining, like wearing a corset around your midriff for 24 hours a day. Also, the material was itchy and its presence obvious under the first 10 outfits I tried on. How the hell did I let this happen?

With no way out, I hauled myself out of bed the next morning at 7:30 and dragged myself to the office. That day was tough and long. I counted down the patients until the day was done. Any difficult parent or screaming child annoyed me. The following day, I was back in the operating room and not feeling that much better. In character, I soldiered on through and all the cases went perfectly. I garnered sympathy only from the scrub nurses who knew me well and who were shocked to see me back so soon.

At one-week post-op, I was in Dr. Gayle's office to have the bandages removed. Somehow, despite showering with soap every day, the binding tape was still 100 percent adhered to my skin. The process of removing it was like having a thousand super-glue Band-aids ripped off all at once. *And now for the big reveal...*underneath, things did not look so pretty. My skin was bruised and gnarly with deep imprints from the binder.

"Looks exactly how it's supposed to look," he smiled approvingly, adding, *"worst case, we may need to do a tummy tuck later. Remember, you did have three children. That stretches the skin... A LOT."*

I mean, seriously?

Dr. Gayle did not like the rippling effect that the abdominal binder had on my wound healing. He advised me to purchase online a piece of lingerie from *Design Veronique*, a California-based company that specializes in post-surgical sexy body wear. For 99 bucks, I bought a lacy black one-piece that I wore for a few weeks and never put on again. For the next many nights, I was tortured by the tightness of this garment. Also, I had temporary loss of normal sensation and the skin looked lumpy and bumpy to me. It was not the enviable flat tummy I was shooting for.

I cried a few times in the shower, my favorite place. I was losing ground. When you are feeling so disappointed in the faults of your own body, it's nearly impossible to accept that someone else can still find you appealing. Pregnancy pales in comparison to this change. With pregnancy, there are unsightly elements like stretch marks and hemorrhoids and extra fat. But, there is still objective beauty in the metamorphosis that occurs when creating a life. Also, at the end, albeit slowly and with hard work, your body can return to its prior state. That is not necessarily the case after breast cancer. With the help of your surgeon, silicone implants, skin grafts and tattoos, you can eventually recreate a new version of you, but it is not the same. This can make you feel angry. It's hard not to turn around and punish the person in your life who cares the most. It's even harder to know how to stop once you've started.

Despite my anger at the areas of ugliness, Alex was nobly persistent in his attraction to me. We were both sitting on the couch and he was skimming through my weekend-reading guilty pleasure, *People Magazine*. He stopped on the "Star Tracks" page as I looked over his shoulder to see a picture of two hot models running through the surf in string bikinis. He glanced over at me and commented offhandedly,

"Models are just so weird looking these days. You're way prettier."

My impulse was to get upset, argue and point out all my glaring faults. I thought about shouting,

"Hey, are you blind? Don't you see that I have slits instead

of nipples and scars and grooves where there should be normal smooth skin?"

Amazingly, I didn't. I just looked at him, grinned and replied,

"Thanks, Babes."

"Well, it's true, anyway."

And, he went right back to flipping through the magazine.

The Devil You Know

Sadly, repeat surgeries and rippled torsos are not the only post-cancer joys that await the remission stage of your journey. Tamoxifen citrate is a popular estrogen receptor modulator (SERM). It is used as adjuvant therapy (additional cancer treatment given after the primary treatment to lower the risk that the cancer will come back). It reduces the risk of recurrence as well as cancer mortality. While Tamoxifen is very effective, it also has serious side effects that include stroke and blood clots. The more common side effects are bone pain, nausea, fatigue, headaches, and depression. It can also cause weight gain, aptly dubbed "Tamoxifen tummy." Even worse, it increases your risk of another cancer you really don't want, endometrial cancer.

Somewhere in that tightly folded medication package insert, amongst the extensive list of potential side effects, "endometrial hyperplasia" or overgrowth of the uterine lining is included. It sounds counterintuitive that an anti-estrogen medication would stimulate the uterine lining. In fact, Tamoxifen has modest estrogenic (estrogen-promoting) properties in the uterus. This can lead to some unwanted stuff down the road such as a three-fold increase in the rate of uterine polyps and cancer. Luckily, even with Tamoxifen, the risk of this badness is still very low.[4] In the meantime, there is a practical implication when that extra heaped up lining sloughs off at the end of the month. It regards the type of tampons you need to buy. In my case, only super plus with two Maxipads with wings does the trick. Anything less will NOT hold. I learned this the hard way during a flight to Washington D.C. aboard which I did not have any spare clothes. More than my level of embarrassment, which was significant, I was petrified that I was bleeding to death. Rather than a friendly period, it looked like a massacre had occurred in my uterus. Lesson learned! Next time 'Aunt Flo' comes to town, better be prepared!

Another fun fact: like most other cancer treatments, Tamoxifen can decrease libido. Despite its various drawbacks, no one talks much about them. The oncologist sends a prescription to your pharmacy and you are basically told to ingest one pill daily for the next decade. So, I took the twenty-milligram little white pill for over a year and I never asked any questions. I didn't experience pain or hair loss or constipation, so I counted myself lucky. I could tolerate this. Anyway, I had to.

"And remember, don't skip any days. It's your lifeline."

In comparison to the other options, Tamoxifen sounded benign. It was much less intimidating to me than what Dr. Wasserheit was suggesting, namely shutting down my ovaries or "ovarian ablation." Because the ovaries are the main source of estrogen in premenopausal women, estrogen levels can be reduced by suppressing or eliminating ovarian function. This can be accomplished surgically by removing the ovaries or with drugs (such as Lupron or Zoladex). The side effects of hormone-suppression therapy depend largely on the specific drug or type of treatment. They include bone loss, mood swings, increased risk of heart attack, heart failure, and hyper-cholesterolemia. On the upside, you never get your crazy-heavy period again. At first, Dr. Wasserheit seemed happy enough with the long-term Tamoxifen plan. She mentioned the idea of ovarian suppression, but she wasn't pushing the hard sell.

Midway through my treatment, a large paper was published in a major medical journal examining the effect of adding complete ovarian suppression to the treatment of women with breast cancer.[5] Three-hundred and fifty of these women were premenopausal with advanced disease, just like me. Dr. Wasserheit felt it was time for me to consider a more aggressive long-term treatment plan. She gave me a copy of the *New England Journal of Medicine* article and I promised her I'd read it. I drove around with it on the passenger seat for weeks before finally bringing it inside.

The journal article was technical and difficult to decipher. The results boil down to this:

Pre-menopausal women with hormone-receptor-positive breast cancer who shut down their ovaries prematurely had a higher chance of being cancer-free five years after treatment.

After the release of this research data, Dr. Wasserheit became more anxious. She cared about me. I think she was frightened by the idea of a young-doctor-mother-patient of hers dying in her 30s, especially if there was anything she could offer to prevent it. When I explained my persistent reservations about ovarian shut-down, she pulled me into the hallway. Another female oncologist was standing at her computer writing patient notes. Dr. Wasserheit interrupted her,

"You haven't heard much complaining about Lupron from female patients, RIGHT?"

She looked hesitant to respond.

"Well, I guess not. No, not that I recall recently."

She looked at me and added,

"I think you should at least try it."

This endorsement was feeble and far from convincing. Everything I had read on cancer blogs pointed to the contrary. Here are some of the disconcerting excerpts I found:

"I couldn't take the side effects... serious hot flashes that actually woke me up at night... dizziness, heart palpitations and other symptoms."

"There is no way to sugar coat it... sweat running down my back, chills, insomnia, joint pains to the point I can't walk... moody, emotional, exhausted even after three years."

As much as I craved every single percentage point of survival advantage and as much as I wanted to do anything to avoid leaving my daughters motherless and my husband a widower, I was still scared. So, instead of facing Dr. Wasserheit's disapproval head-on, I did the cowardly thing. I avoided her completely. In that same timeframe, she moved her practice further from my home and work. This confluence of events prompted me to transfer my care to Dr. Subuhee Hussain at White Plains Hospital. The White Plains Hospital cancer center was just down the block from my house, in the same building as I received my radiation treatments. Dr. Hussain had been in practice for over ten years. She was highly-regarded. She was smart and current on all the medical literature and research. When we met, Dr. Hussain also made a plug for the Lupron injections. She, too, wanted to see me live to raise my children. I assured her that I'd consider it fully. I never committed.

In addition to my fear of the ovarian suppression side

effects, I had another concern. Time had passed from the full-on physical assault of having breast cancer and, accordingly, I was supposed to be "back to normal." For some reason, this "normal" didn't feel like me at all. I had a persistent sense of disconnection, like I was an observer in my own life. I was going through the motions of motherhood and wifehood, but I felt numb. The positive emotions were not there. Not so, regarding anger and annoyance. I could feel those two bastards acutely! I still wasn't sad like a typical depressed person. I didn't have trouble getting out of bed in the morning. I never felt hopeless or suicidal. That's why my problem was so difficult to pinpoint. Was it the Tamoxifen or was something else dulling my enjoyment of life? When was the last time I felt truly happy? I couldn't really remember. Had it been that long?

Let me think...

For the first year or so after completing my treatment, I chalked up my constant fatigue and despondence to the prolonged effects of radiation and chemotherapy. I remember asking Dr. Stevens at my six-month radiation follow-up visit.

"Is this normal? Should I feel this way?"

"What isn't normal is going back full time to working as a surgeon right after chemotherapy and then straight through radiation. Your body never had any time to recoup. Therefore, it will take a lot longer."

Then, for months after my father died, I attributed my feeling of emptiness to his recent death. I remember once, sitting in the driveway outside my house, having a hard time going inside. I called Dov.

"Do you ever find yourself crying when you're alone?"

"Not really. Then again, I'm not as sensitive as you."

Two years in, I was still lost inside. At work, I fought hard to be upbeat and personable. At home, my short-temper and frustration strained my marriage. This stealing of my emotional well-being was gradual and insidious and basically undetectable, even to my closest friends. On a trip to Puerto Rico to meet up with a long-time friend from college, she became infuriated at the way I was constantly snapping at Alex. I kept trying to get her alone, so I could tell her that I was sinking in quicksand and didn't understand why. I never got the chance. She chastised me for under-appreciating my three wonderful children, awesome job, spacious home and loving spouse. She thought I didn't appreciate what a daily struggle life could be.

Back in Westchester, there was a woman named Meirav whose breast cancer diagnosis dovetailed mine. I befriended her. We spent a lot of time together during treatment, comparing notes. She was always one step behind me on the shitty cancer road. When I was doing chemo, she was starting oncologic surgery. When she finished chemo, I was starting radiation. She absolutely *hated* Tamoxifen. She said it made her feel "crummy" and "messed up." She quickly quit it for another option, Exemestane. But unlike me, she was post-menopausal. In comparison, I thought I tolerated Tamoxifen well. To me, it was the devil I knew. I didn't feel spectacular. However, I could manage my life on it. Stabilized back at work, I was reluctant to change any medications that might upset my equilibrium.

So, I plugged away. For several more months, I continued bottling my despondence deep inside. Then, one night, I was lying on the bottom bunk bed in Scarlett's room. I watched her sleeping next to me, her scrumptious cheeks and chiseled nose, the rise and fall of her chest and the smell of her sweet breath.

And, instead of pure bliss, I felt nothing. It was at that moment that I realized I had slipped ever so gently into depression and that I needed a way out.

As I mentioned, over the course of my ordeal, I had been given several prescriptions for antidepressants. They all remained tucked in the secret zippered-fold of my wallet. I hated the idea of daily dependence on yet another pill. The next morning, I filled my first prescription for the antidepressant Lexapro. Two weeks later, I was reminded of what I had been missing. As I danced in Scarlett's bedroom, lights dimmed, jamming to the latest Ariana Grande tune, I felt joy. Several weeks after that, I marched into Dr. Hussain's office.

"I am ready."

"Ready for what?"

"Ready to try out my Lupron shot. Ready to take a chance so I can be there longer for my family."

"It's too late. That ship sailed a long time ago."

"Wait, for what? Since when?"

"Well, there is definitely no data to support the utility of starting ovarian suppression two years after the completion of chemotherapy. It would be purely experimental. I don't think it's worth the risk. Anyway, you made your decision a long time ago."

"I did? Why have I been torturing myself all this time?"

"I don't know. You can stop now."

And just like that, POOF, the agonizing was over.

Road Trip!

My previous visit to Dr. Gayle had been disappointing. He thought that the skin overlying the left implant had signs of long-term radiation-induced changes. This meant it was thinner and fibrotic. He did not think nipple reconstruction on that side was a good option. Even worse, he was now concerned about another complication called "implant exposure." In this situation, the tissue overlying the implant breaks down to the point that a secondary surgery is often necessary to repair it. This other surgery involves the rotation of a skin-muscle flap. It's a big deal when it happens. It is another serious surgery with a prolonged recovery and long scar. Dr. Gayle thought this complication was unlikely to happen. But, he wanted to avoid further incisions and manipulation of the skin in that area. Neither of us wanted to take any risk.

Acute cutaneous reactions to radiation therapy are common. They typically start 1-2 weeks after the start of radiation and last through its duration. The severity of these skin changes ranges from mild redness to complete skin ulceration and sloughing. Radiation can also cause burns. Having ignored proper skin care guidelines, I was sure I'd have these problems. Yet, throughout my entire treatment course, my skin was normal and healthy. If not for the debilitating fatigue, I would have been convinced that the radiation techs had forgotten to turn on the machine. It didn't occur to me to worry about late-stage changes. Back then, concerns far into the future were still a luxury to me. Now, I was standing in Dr. Gayle's office as he pinched the skin over my left and right implants.

"See the difference? There's just no give on this side."

"So, what are my options now?"

"You can tattoo the left and reconstruct the right. Or, you can tattoo them both," he replied.

"Well, I've gone without nipples this long. Do I really need them again?"

He looked at me. *"That's a question only you can answer."*

I called Alex on the long familiar drive home from Brooklyn.

"I think this isn't such bad news. I'll just go ahead with the tattooing on both sides and be done with all of this."

There was an extremely long pause after I told him. I thought we'd been disconnected.

"Hello, are you there?"

"Yes, I'm still here."

"Why are you so quiet?"

"I'm processing."

"Processing what? Are you upset?"

"I don't want to say anything. It's your body and your decision. I just thought you'd want... you know... ultimately... to be complete again."

"You mean I'd want that or you would???"

I started to get angry again and indignant, but I managed to stop myself. Alex's disappointment really surprised me. He was much more upset than I expected. At first, I struggled to understand why. Unsettling questions began to swirl around in my thoughts. Alex's unfaltering attraction to me was something I relied on as a formidable truth. What if it was a lie? Eventually, I calmed myself down. I realized that all the recent changes that had scarred me emotionally and physically had impacted him too. It was normal and fair for him to care about the final anatomical product.

On the other hand, what choice did I have?

Ultimately, without the possibility of nipple symmetry, I thought the option of unilateral reconstruction wasn't worth it. It was time to travel to Finksburg to meet Vinnie.

Road Trip!

For working mothers, one of the most precious commodities we have is time. We just don't have enough of it and we can't get more of it. That is why I felt especially grateful when my hardworking friends Karen and Debbie offered to take two days off from their busy work schedules to drive with me to Maryland. I had decided that I needed some closure. By closure, I mean nipples.

I picked up Karen and Debbie and loaded my Subaru with various snacks and drinks for the ride. As we backed out of my driveway, "Sweet Home Alabama" blasted in the background. Our exit from White Plains would have been so much cooler in a cherry red convertible with leather seats and the top down. I wish I could have justified the splurge.

Our drive down to Maryland was filled with bubbly conversation about our jobs, our husbands and our children's talents and struggles. Deeper into South Jersey, we talked about our childhoods, our sibling-in-law interactions, and our college boyfriends. With my two girlfriends on the open road, I felt like myself again. It was cathartic and invigorating, especially because it would culminate in my arrival at Little Vinnies.

By the time we arrived in Maryland, it was dark. I had booked a one-night stay in the nearby town of Westminster at a place called "The Boston Inn." The tiny road leading to the Inn was deserted and winding, straight out of a horror flick. After twenty nail-biting minutes on that road, we arrived safely and unloaded into our first-floor room. It was a basic, acceptably clean motel, unlike its name suggested. Two bottles of wine later, we were all feeling happy. There were no screaming kids, no "Please Mommy just one more story," no one complaining, "I don't want to go to bed!" It was heavenly, relaxing and quiet. Maybe a bit too quiet. Karen was convinced we'd be murdered in our sleep. A few hours later, despite her fears, the three of us passed out crisscrossed on the beds. In the morning, we were still alive, though a tad hungover.

We grabbed a quick brunch and arrived at the strip mall storefront housing Little Vinnies. As promised, it was the complete tattoo parlor experience. There were multiple booths off the main waiting area in which you could hear the buzzing of electric needles. After a short wait, out came Vinnie in his goatee and Fedora, just as I had pictured him. We were ushered into his private office which was recently remodeled. On the floor, there lay a black and white tiger rug. Debbie and Karen plopped down on the long white leather couch.

"Do you mind if I have my assistant take some photographs?"

My discomfort at stripping down in front of "medical" strangers had long been abandoned. I didn't hesitate to show my scars to Vinnie and my friends because I wasn't ashamed.

Vinnie eyed me carefully. He took some measurements and

looked at me from various angles. I wasn't prepared for what he said next.

"I can't do it. You won't be happy. Your left implant is rotated. I'm sure of it."

"It is?"

Vinnie was absolutely convinced that the only remedy was surgical correction. He was impressively knowledgeable having logged many hours of in the operating room observing implant surgeries with a local plastic surgeon.

"Here, let me show you."

He wheeled his chair over to the desk and pulled out a clear, rectangular plastic box with two silicone nipples inside.

"May I?"

"Yup, go right ahead."

"So, the tattoos would be positioned, here and here." He applied the fake nipples to my skin and they stuck temporarily.

He directed me towards a full-length mirror.

"You see, to put it bluntly, the headlights would be shining in different directions."

I saw his point. I asked Vinnie to take a few pictures on my phone. Then, I excused myself to call Dr. Gayle. Uncharacteristically, he picked up his cell. I explained the situation, that I was all the way in Finksburg. I texted him the images.

"I do not think the implant could have rotated. But, you'll have to come back to see me in person."

"Of course. Ok. I get it."

I hung up with Dr. Gayle and walked back to Vinnie's office. Karen and Debbie were waiting patiently.

"I have to go back."

I kept it cool while my heart was sinking. No closure for me. Not today, at least.

Vinnie handed me the box.

"I'm sorry. You can keep these, to show your surgeon."

"Excellent, thanks. I'll do that."

The three of us returned to the car. I placed my box of nipples in the glove compartment. We drove for an hour in silence. What was there to say?

Karen and Debbie waited for my meltdown. It never came.

"Do you mind if we stop in Allentown? I want to show you where I grew up."

"Sure, whatever you need."

Allentown is the small town in Pennsylvania where I lived until I was fourteen. It was a small detour off the route back to White Plains. On the way, we passed by the endless corn fields that I remembered from my youth. Off Route 22, just past the Lehigh Valley Mall, I exited onto Cedar Crest Blvd. A few blocks later, I turned left onto Arch Street and parked in front of 1231 North Arch Street, the home my mother designed and built over three and half decades ago. The house had been neglected over the years. The once carefully manicured landscaping was overgrown and half-dead. The dark brown shutters looked shabby. The paint on the basketball hoop at the end of the driveway, that my parents had erected when I was ten, was peeling and the net was torn.

It all felt so familiar and yet so much had changed.

I stood there in silence for a while, allowing all childhood memories to dance around in my mind: kite flying in the empty lot down the block, scootering with J.J. without a helmet down the steep hill, that time I ran away from home with my favorite toys wrapped in a sheet until my father found me down the block on his return from work.

Back in the car and on the road, it was Debbie who asked.

"Aren't you going to freak out? We came all this way just to be turned away without doing anything."

"I know I should. I just can't."

"Why not? I would."

"At this point, I have to roll with the punches. There is no other choice, or I'll go crazy. Thank you, though, for being here, for coming with me. I know how impossible it is to take off work. I really appreciate it, a lot."

At 10:30 pm, when I arrived back home after nine hours of driving in two days, I was tired and defeated. I crawled into bed where Alex was still awake.

"The trip was a bust. I can't believe it."

"I know Babes, it stinks. It really does. It will happen. Eventually, you'll be back... and I'd like it, if next time, we could go together."

"Really? You would want to? I thought the whole idea of nipple tattooing might weird you out."

"Well, I wouldn't necessarily watch it being done. I would go to be there with you, as a team."

I had made this mistake before, wrongly assuming it was better to spare him from something than to allow him to be a part of it. In truth, I hadn't even asked him if he wanted to come with me. I had labeled it as a girl's trip without giving him the option of coming.

"I had this idea, of renting motorcycles and buying bikers jackets and riding down to Maryland together."

I smiled. Alex's image was touching and unexpected.

"You did? I had no idea."

"Yes. You never gave me the chance to tell you."

"I'm sorry, let's go to sleep. We can talk about it in the morning."

I fell asleep quickly that night, exhausted from all the driving. I had the most wonderful dream: Hitting the open road, riding my hog with Alex alongside me in matching black leather gear. I had on my favorite pink lipstick, dangling earrings, and big black sunglasses. On my head was this bright red bandana that looked so cool. And this time, I was wearing it by choice.

The Further Redistribution of Fat

Weeks later, back at Dr. Gayle's office, I asked if there was any way he would reconsider bilateral nipple reconstruction. I explained about Alex's reaction and my trip to Little Vinnies. Dr. Gayle suggested that further fat injections may improve the health of the radiated skin. It could also help reduce the risk of implant exposure. He couldn't make any promises about the viability of a skin graft on that side. We decided to table the discussion and proceed with repeat fat grafting for now. He adamantly disagreed with Vinnie's claim that the implant had rotated. He wiggled my left breast to demonstrate how tightly it sat in its pocket. Yet he did agree that there was asymmetry and that Vinnie was the expert on tattooing outcomes.

"If he doesn't think it would look good, I'm sure he's right."

I wasn't sure where this comment left me. In the meantime, I refocused on preventing complications and improving contours.

As you've probably figured out by now, there are few benefits to having breast cancer. Constant fear of an untimely death is not one of them. The repeated need to suck out body fat from unwanted areas and re-inject it into your boobs? Now *that's* an appealing concept.

When Dr. Gayle first laid out my long-term strategy for reconstruction after bilateral mastectomy, I was distraught. The number of steps and future surgeries seemed unthinkable to a person who had never so much as broken a pinkie finger. And how would this jive with the eventual return to my crazy work schedule? There were so many appointments, pre-op and post-op, with countless trips from Westchester to the hospital in Brooklyn. It was a hassle fighting traffic back and forth from Manhattan over the Triboro Bridge to the Brooklyn-Queens Expressway. If not for my staunch loyalty to the breast team there and my enjoyment of the post-visit dinner dates with Natalie, I would never have traveled that far for medical care.

Time has a way of easing you into realities that once seemed impossible to fathom.

Fat grafting, also called autologous fat transfer, is the process of removing fat tissue from a part of the body by liposuction (usually thighs, belly, and buttocks). The tissue is then processed into liquid and injected into the breast area. Like the currently popular "body contouring" procedure, the goal is to improve the shape of the underlying tissue. In contrast, though, the purpose of fat grafting after bilateral mastectomy and radiation is to improve the quality of the overlying damaged skin. It is also used to fill various divots and hollows to recreate the natural curves of the breast. This lofty goal sounds less vain than the desire to achieve a sculpted Khloe-Kardashian-like shape. That doesn't mean you can't enjoy the results just the same.

As I discovered previously, recovery from this surgery, though unpleasant, is not unbearable. Initially, though, it is quite disgusting. The tumescent solution, a mixture of dilute lidocaine (anesthetic) and epinephrine (vasoconstrictor), is injected into the harvest site to decrease post-operative pain and bleeding. Unfortunately, in the wise words of Shrek the ogre:

"What goes in must come out."

So, the inserted liquid slowly extrudes out of the incision sites over the first few days. That means you better lay lots of padding down on your sheets and really protect your comforter. Otherwise, you'll have some nasty ass stains. It's also hard to hide from your kids. Even though I'm a proponent of openness, no child wants to know that their mother is oozing brown/yellow liquid through her skin. It's creepy.

When I saw Dr. Gayle prior to my second fat grafting surgery, he casually questioned,

"Where will I find fat to suck out this time?"

Worried that he would run into a supply issue, I took his offhanded comment as an edict to eat more... more junk, that is. I mean, tons more. Let me just say that my entire life, I have been careful with what I consume. For the first fat transfer, I didn't have a chance to prime my fat stores. Now almost a full year later, I would come prepared. Since I had planned the operation several months out, I had plenty of time to plump up. And I did. I indulged in all available pastry offerings and many varieties of carbohydrates. After all, what did I have to lose, except my self-control? I mistakenly reasoned that whatever fat I ingested now was helping my cause later, bettering my chances at the best skin and breast results. To a degree, I was correct. When I emerged from anesthesia after the second transfer, I hazily remember Dr. Gayle remarking,

"Wow, I was NOT expecting you to have that much fat!"

Ok, good...I guess. Notwithstanding the insult, I was pleased.

The fat transfer was a swimming success. It filled in most of the defects and gave me a better cleavage line. With the continued feathering of fat overlying the implant, the health of my radiated skin improved drastically. The skin went from thin and bluish, through which I could easily palpate the button on my implant (not good) to more normal-appearing with less rippling when I lifted my arm (better). Most importantly, it got rid of my rapidly expanding muffin top, the inconvenient fat that spills over the waist of your undersized jeans. It also addressed the jiggle between my inner thighs that I have hated since I was a teenager.

There are several dangers in believing that you can re-appropriate any newly acquired fat at will and that whatever caloric crap you eat can later be sucked out by your plastic surgeon. For one, liposuction only really takes care of limited target areas. As I said, the most common donor sites for fat transfer for breast reconstruction are the abdomen and inner thigh. The surgeon is not going to spend hours rooting around in other places unless you are willing to pay for it, separately.

Liposuction is great for fitting into jeans and wearing cute belts, but it doesn't address face fat. This means, if you pig out for months, your face will get fat. Like depression, it's an insidious thing that happens very sneakily. At first, I thought I kept stumbling into bad lighting or glancing into screwy mirrors. Maybe I needed to upgrade my iPhone camera? It was easy to deceive myself because my stomach was flat and my waist was small. Eventually, I started to realize that my face was looking fat consistently, and in all settings, and with every camera and in EVERY picture. My friends weren't any help in forcing me to accept reality and neither was Alex. When I asked him if I was gaining too much weight, he only answered that I could consider toning my legs a bit... that is, only if it was bothering ME. Oh, by the way, did I mention that fat can grow back?

There is also the issue of fat necrosis. Fat necrosis occurs when the blood supply to the fat is inadequate. The fat cells die and as they die, they release fatty acids and other chemicals that cause inflammation and swelling and sometimes pain. Usually, the fat necrosis presents as a non-tender lump. I have a vague recollection that somewhere back in time, Dr. Gayle warned me about this. He advised me that one of the downsides of fat injection was that fat necrosis can feel very much like cancer. This would be especially alarming to a female surgeon who found her big breast cancer lump while randomly poking around at herself one night.

For some reason, my mind filed away his cautioning under "things to forget completely."

Several months later, I was sitting in a Grand Rounds lecture at Beth Israel, a bit bored. I started tapping my fingers on my chest and inadvertently discovered multiple small hard nodules above my left clavicle that didn't belong there. As I sat listening to the lecture on "New Techniques in the Treatment of Obstructive Sleep Apnea," a familiar feeling of anxiety began to consume me. Alarmed, I ran out into the hallway to call Natalie.

She reassured me with the cursory, *"I'm sure it's nothing."*

Yeah, I've heard that one before!

Natalie was quick to add, *"Let me squeeze you in for an ultrasound ASAP just to check."*

SHIT!

After my office hours the next day, I drove back to Brooklyn in a sweat. I did not tell Alex because I didn't know what to say...

"Hey honey, I may really be dying this time around."

I remember looking out at the water along the Belt Parkway while driving and promising God what a better person I'd become if He would just let this be nothing. I imagined my eulogy...again. This time, with each family member speaking separately.

My oncologist's words, *"You will be high risk for recurrence for the rest of your life,"* stuck in my head.

When I reached the Maimonides Breast Center, I was quickly ushered in by Natalie's ultrasound technician, Sara. She squirted a wad of warm lube on my chest and asked a bunch of cryptic questions.

"So where exactly do you feel it?"

"Over here."

"Oh, so right here."

"Yes."

"Here? Here where I'm pointing?"

"Yes, yes there."

"What about these other areas?"

"There are other areas too?"

I looked at the screen as she loomed over a suspicious shadow. My heart sunk. She snapped several pictures from different angles and typed rapidly into the computer.

"Ok, I think I have enough images. I'll be right back."

Then she excused herself to go talk to Natalie.

As I lay there on the table, I was sure it was cancer again. It seemed like an eternity before Sara returned with Natalie.

As she opened her mouth to speak, I slipped in one last "Hail Mary" in my mind.

"It's all ok... classic fat necrosis."

"Fat necrosis. Are you sure? Positively sure?"

"I am sure."

"Well damnit, maybe he should have warned me!"

Five months later, I was back again in Dr. Gayle's office for a follow-up. Pleased so far with my relatively low rate of fat resorption, he predicted this third time may be my last ride on the merry-go-round. I was faced with the greatest decision of all: from where should I take the fat? I won't go into the details of my decision because my friends and family will likely be reading this and there are some secrets best left untold. Let's just say, I chose wisely.

At my most recent post-op visit, Dr. Gayle looked proud of his work.

"Overall, I am pleased with your results. I think this really is the last time we needed to do this. At least, for the foreseeable future."

It was bizarre to near the end of the long trek to the summit of my breast recon-Everest. I was glad, although not as relieved as I expected. It was just the year before that I was potentially facing another major surgery with a flap rotation. The year before that, I was trudging through cancer and chemo and hair loss. Now, I was looking good.

Maybe my lack of relief was because I still had no nipples. I know, hard to believe, but true. Or was I afraid to be done? After I stopped focusing on all the surgical steps, I'd have to start worrying about recurrence. I think it was another reason. I realized that there were no more free passes, no cupcakes with cream cheese frosting or Krispy Kreme doughnuts or tubs of chocolate cookie dough ice cream. HOLY CRAP. I needed to start dieting immediately! Dieting and exercising. I started breathing rapidly. My head was getting fuzzy and I felt faint. I had just canceled my gym membership for lack of use! Then, I took a deep chakra breath and remembered that, at least, I still have plenty of full body Spanxs in my drawer.

Wearing Heels Again

About ten months before I discovered the pesky cancerous lump, I started noticing that my right big toe was hurting whenever I wore high heels. For the first several months, I shrugged off the persistent tenderness and wrongly assumed that I'd banged it somehow. I theorized that whatever the mechanism of injury, it would be sure to heal on its own. I treated it exactly as seriously as the gnawing tooth pain that I began to feel about two months into my year of general surgery internship: with cavalier neglect.

During internship, I was 29 years old and consumed with the mission of becoming a doctor, at the expense of all else. I ignored the nagging discomfort in my right lower jaw for several weeks. By late fall of 2004, I started requiring Tylenol every four to six hours to calm the throbbing pain. With hundred-hour work weeks, I never made the time to see a proper dentist. By mid-November, nothing over-the-counter was working. I finally scheduled a dental examination with x-rays. By then I was told that my two bottom molars were already past the point of salvation, even with a root canal. The following week, I had these two teeth pulled by an oral surgery resident, Snehal

Patel, under IV sedation in the Columbia Hospital dental clinic. This was my first experience under anesthesia, ever.

Almost 10 years later, I was again trying to ignore the mounting and exquisite tenderness in my right big toe during any attempt at extension or flexion. After numerous months of exclusively wearing my purple Dansko clogs, I became desperate. There were too many upcoming social events on my calendar for which I wanted to pair an elegant long dress with sexy shoes. Flats simply wouldn't do.

Trusting there was an easy explanation and solution to my problem, I went to see an orthopedic surgeon. In the waiting room, I couldn't help noticing that I was several decades younger than the other patients. I didn't suspect then that this experience would portend the reality ahead.

Dr. Hoisington called me into his office and examined my foot thoroughly, bending and twisting my ankles and toes. Ouch. He then ordered an x-ray of my foot.

"It's osteoporosis of the right proximal first metatarsal joint. That's your big toe."

"Huh? I'm only 37. Isn't that a disease of old people?"

"Well typically, for most people, yes, but no, not in your case."

"Ok then. Well, what should we do to cure it?"

"There are several choices, none of them fully curative. First, we could start steroid injections and see how that goes. Or, if it eventually becomes much worse and unbearably painful, you could consider surgery. I wouldn't recommend it and anyway, the problem is still likely to recur."

"So, what do you recommend?"

"I suggest you just never wear heels again."

"Never?" I asked in disbelief

"Yes. Never."

"Like, never ever?" I nearly shouted

"Never, ever again."

I left his office in a bad state. Flash back to my twenties... I trekked all over the streets of Manhattan in my favorite red peep-toe heels. At the time, I thought I was sacrificing comfort for beauty. It never occurred to me that I could be causing permanent damage to my feet. Why had I been so stupid? If only I had known. I would have carried my fancy shoes in a tote bag and walked around in sneakers.

Weeks later, still reeling from the news of my toe's chronic ailment, I was walking with Tiffany and lamenting. It was exactly five days before my father's cancer discovery and three weeks before my own.

"I know I should feel lucky that this is literally my only health problem. But, I just cannot get over this big toe shit-tuation. How will I ever look good in a midi-skirt again?"

More bothersome to me than my new shoe restriction was the idea that I had a problem that would never go away. Ignorant of the devastating news I would soon face, I felt livid. I was simply too young and healthy for a chronic medical condition. I just couldn't accept it.

Tiffany looked at me with genuine sympathy,

"Tali, that really sucks." She cocked her head and made her sorry-for-you face. I shuffled home unhappily in black ballet slippers.

This September, I ventured into DSW shoe warehouse in the Crossroads Shopping Center. I was desperate to purchase something nice for the holidays. In addition to being holy and filled with solemn prayer and repentance, the Jewish High Holidays are a forum to display your most impressive fashion ensembles. Even while intending to concentrate on a higher purpose, most of our eyes wander around the temple sanctuary checking out each other's hats and dresses. Of course, shoes are the key element to tying the whole outfit together.

My first post-treatment Rosh Hashanah was especially important for me. Still sporting my cropped hairdo, I knew many people would be cocking their heads to catch a surreptitious glimpse of the young female doctor who had a baby, cancer, and lost her hair and her beloved father all in the previous year. That woman was me and I was determined to find the right shoes for the occasion. I wove through the long aisle of footwear, never daring to move beyond the low wedge heel section. Then, out of the corner of my eye, in the forbidden display, I spotted a beautiful faux snake-skin pair of dark maroon-colored lovelies. I didn't dare...but I did. And the miracle that occurred as I slipped my right foot into that medium-heeled shoe was that it didn't hurt, not one bit.

The following week, I eagerly wore my most stunning multicolored Parisian peacock-like dress. I walked toward the synagogue entrance with perfectly applied makeup and turquoise earrings, with my head held high and with my feet in heels.

On that day, I prayed hard for my health and for that of my family. I was beginning to see beyond my dread of the dormant beast that is my cancer. I envisioned myself one day walking down the streets of New York or the hallowed halls of my hospital in a new pair of three-inch-heel pointy-toe Jimmy Choo stilettos. In the distance, there lay a truly healed, stronger, fiercer me.

The Bucket List

"So how bad are my odds, really?" is the question I'm compelled to ask at every oncologic check-up and check-in. Inevitably, the response is:

"Well, we hope you're cured."

"Could you be more explicit?"

"I guess, I'd say, you should live your life... but I wouldn't hold off on your bucket list."

Hearing that advice from a doctor whose entire patient population has cancer is not reassuring; it's damn petrifying. It's also confusing, leaving so many questions unanswered. Afterwards, trying to reconcile the two life approaches is impossible. Anyway, which bucket list are we talking about? The I'm-gonna-die-soon, chuck-it-all and move to a hut in Tahiti one or my more pressing top wish to sleep through the night uninterrupted and wake up in the morning with no kids in my bed? Both seemed equally unachievable at this point. And, what is the likely time course for me? Imminent death or you may not live to see your grandchildren? Either option sucks, but in the first case, things become clearer.

If you are going to die soon, you gotta make big moves. Sell your big expensive house with a mortgage and property taxes you can't afford. Pull your kids out of school and fly to Disney World for a week to spend tea time with the princesses. Hock all your jewelry and buy a speedboat. Well, maybe not that. The kids might want some mementos, and anyway I didn't have that much jewelry. Whatever it is, you need to get serious, fast. You need to ask the hard questions. How will your husband raise the kids alone? We depended on our dual-income. How will they live? I never bought life insurance and now I don't qualify. Some ambitious women try to find their own replacements, women to marry their husbands and raise their kids when they are gone. Knowing Alex, he'd be super peeved if I tried to be that controlling.

The general sense I got was that it was looking likely that I had some good years ahead of me. It wasn't time to find new-Mommy just yet. How would I know when the final countdown started? Would anybody have the guts to tell me?

One of the challenges of advance staged breast cancer with bilateral mastectomy is that there are no reliable surveillance methods. In the case of lumpectomy or unilateral mastectomy, follow-up mammography, ultrasonography, MRI or PET may be used to increase detection of recurrence at an early stage. But, once you have no breast tissue, there is no recommended imaging studies to confirm that you remain cancer free. There are no accurate blood tests either. This was a hard concept for me to wrap my head around.

Early on, when I pressed Dr. Wasserheit on this issue, she assured me that I would be closely monitored. This included regularly scheduled visits every three to four months to continue for the foreseeable future.

"Basically, I just wait for something bad to happen?" I asked in disbelief.

"*No. You try not to think about it. Just don't ignore any symptoms either.*"

This advice is not so simple to follow. In practice, it is tough deciphering the metastatic symptoms from the normal common ones. Take a cough for example, which has so many causes. How can you tell when it's a recurrence or just a bad cold? When is a headache a giant tumor in your brain or just a migraine acting up? Generally, the answer lies in severity, persistence, and escalation. This means if you are not hacking up a lung or having seizures and your problem resolves on its own in two days, most likely it's not cancer.

Whenever I begin to panic over a specific symptom, I typically hear Arnold Schwarzenegger's voice in my head reassuring me,

"*It's not a tumah.*"

To date, there have been three instances when I really thought,

"*Oh God, it is a 'tumah!*'"

The three associated symptoms were the classic cancer trifecta: cough, headache and bone pain. In each of these cases, before I freaked out, I checked that my problem met the criterion above. In all instances, the answer was a resounding, "yes."

Last year, I developed progressive severe lower back pain lasting several days. By the third day, I found myself lying on the hard floor in my office curled up in a ball, moaning, in-between patients. I kept waiting for escalating signs such as foot drop (a gait abnormality in which the foot drags due to nerve or muscle weakness) because my hairdresser's sister had discovered her spinal metastasis that way. Fortunately, that never happened. Turns out, I was just severely constipated again from eating too much chopped liver, which is filled with iron.

Six months ago, I had a horrible dry hacking cough that was so severe I had to break OR scrub every 10 minutes. The force of the cough was so strong, I vomited blood-tinged phlegm a few times throughout the day. Midway through a course of self-prescribed antibiotics and steroids, I was unimproved. I was about to call my oncologist to order a chest x-ray when the symptoms went away. A few days later, my entire family started coughing. I guess it was just a virus.

Most recently, I developed an excruciating headache that lasted for four days. The pain awakened me from sleep. It was not relieved by Extra Strength Tylenol, Excedrin or the migraine pills that I still had in my medicine cabinet from seven years prior. This time, I really thought I was done for. I spent hundreds of dollars out of pocket getting a fancy brain MRI at a local facility. Thank God, it was normal. As it turned out, I just needed migraine medicine that wasn't expired. I was not always like this. Before cancer, I was the opposite of a hypochondriac. I used to ignore all those little signals from my body telling me something was wrong. I just assumed everything would resolve eventually. Now, it was hard not to be alarmed.

Eventually, the business of life distracts you. You still have episodic scares, but otherwise, you find yourself preoccupied with normal things like carpool and ballet practice. You worry why one of your kids can't do cartwheels, the other struggles with math and the youngest hits her classmates.

In addition to affecting your health, there is an expectation that cancer should make you recalibrate your life. It should force you to prioritize what is important, like family and friends. And it does, for a while. With time though, once the fear of imminent death subsides, you fall back into your regular patterns.

My Aunt Ziva came to visit from Israel during the worst of it all. My father was in awful shape and I was besieged with doubt regarding the future of my health. Ziva and I talked in the sunny atrium of Kessler Rehabilitation Center, where my father was a patient. Despite the institution's name, by then, my father had no hope of recovery. He was no longer cognitively or verbally fluent, his once sturdy six-foot frame slumped in a tabled wheelchair. Intermittently, he would burst out screaming,

"Pain, pain."

Ziva took me away into the corner. She looked me dead in the eyes.

"I'm worried about you. You are too stressed."

"It's part of my DNA."

"Tell me, what are the things you love to do in life, I mean except work?

"I'm...not sure."

"Well, you need to find out what they are, soon. And you need to start doing more of them."

It was ironic getting advice about indulgence from a woman who had lived a relatively austere life. Ziva was born in Romania and emigrated to Israel with her brother and parents in the 60s. They lived in the poor Arab-Israeli town of Ramallah. She had met my uncle Danny while studying chemistry at Hebrew University in Jerusalem. Danny was a kind, soft-spoken, intelligent man from a prominent rabbinical family. She was a tall, stunning woman with bright blue eyes. My uncle had pursued her fervently until she acquiesced to marry him. They had a wonderful marriage and raised five children together in a city named Rechovot which means "wide expanses" based on Genesis 26:22:

He named it Rehoboth, saying, "Now the LORD hath given us room and we will flourish in the land.[6]*"*

Despite the city's expanse, they had reared their family of seven in a small four-bedroom apartment. Money was tight. In terms of material things, there was never excess. Finally, in their 50s, the financial strains started to relax. The sad irony was that when we spoke, Ziva herself was already harboring a deadly malignancy. She just didn't know it yet. Our conversation was still theoretical for her. Three months later, she would discover her own fatal truth: stage IV metastatic lung cancer (in a non-smoker). The following summer, Ziva died at the young age of 63, leaving her loving husband, devastated children, and many young grandchildren to mourn her loss.

My discussion with Ziva in the atrium haunted me after her death. By then, I was almost two years out of treatment and back to the juggling act of the professional working mother's life. I still wasn't sure I had the right answers, but I did feel it was finally time to make my list.

-Eating fresh ikura with quail egg

-Slipping back under the covers when the kids leave for school

-Scuba diving along a pristine reef in warm water

-Connecting with my young patients and their parents

-Vacationing alone with Alex somewhere beautiful

-Going out for dinner and drinks with my closest girlfriends

-Taking extra-long hot steamy showers

-Sitting down to movie night on our deep L-shaped couch with a bowl of buttered popcorn

-Sipping sangria on the back porch in the summer

-Blasting the Lumineers on Pandora while finishing patient charts

-Drinking cold brew coffee concentrate with almond milk on ice

-Watching Juliette, Scarlett, and Milla dancing in their underwear

-White wooden built-in bookshelves in my family room

-Wearing multilayered necklaces

-Roasting marshmallows over a fire-pit

-Walking barefoot on soft sandy beaches

-Enjoying snuggle-time with the girls

When I looked at my list carefully, I realized my carpe diem is about the little things. It is about the stolen moments of bliss and selfishness that make daily life more pleasurable. This is *my* answer to Ziva's question. This is what makes *me* happy.

As for my bucket list, I made that one too. I keep it folded up in an envelope, buried deep in my nightstand drawer. And though I'll always know where to find it, I'm determined never to need to open it.

Afterwards

Recently, my friend Lisa commented on my post-cancer look.

"You know you're edgier, more daring... than when I first met you."

"It's the short hair."

"No, it's not. It's everything. It's your whole package. Before you were stylish but more conservative. Now, you are different, gutsier, more of a risk taker."

I attribute my new perceived coolness to my hair stylist Michelle. I first met her in Tuckahoe at an upscale salon. Before finding her, I sent out a group email to my friends asking for reliable recommendations. I was searching for someone talented at cutting short hair who wouldn't make me look like a teenage boy. I found Michelle. We formed an immediate connection. Heavily accented and Irish-born, she is in her mid-twenties with a green four-leaf-clover tattoo. She is the key to my ever-evolving colors, low-lights and pixie cuts. In October, we boldly experiment with different versions of pink. I even followed her all the way to the Bronx!

Why?

I think I know. Cancer changed me profoundly, physically and emotionally. As a physician, it opened my eyes to the vulnerability of the patient experience, the confusion, the fear and the uncertainty. I can't say that my turn on the operating table is what made me empathetic. I always was. I took care of babies, children, and teenagers, in addition to managing their terrified parents. I already recognized that my young patients were scared and defenseless. However, all my surgeries and treatments provided me with a unique dual perspective. Without them, I would not have gained this insight.

Afterwards, I was thrust back out in the world appearing deceptively unscathed. Fundamentally, I was still the same human being, but I needed to mark the transformation. Michelle held the key to my new normal. I did not want to go back to my long ponytails and stick-straight blow-outs. Breast cancer bitch-slapped me. There is no hiding from it. But I am still standing. My short hair makes me feel brazen, like a strong female warrior ready for battle. Whenever it starts growing, I get this itch to chop it off, to dye it or bleach it white-blond to the tips.

When I rise out of Michelle's swivel chair, the mantra in my head grows louder again.

"I am a surgeon, wife, mother, and cancer dragon slayer."

Acknowledgments

To Jordana White, my amazing editor who took on this project over sushi after parent teacher conferences. For having faith in this project. For diligently reworking, remodeling and restructuring my words into a wonderfully coherent kick-ass tale.

To Miriam Shaviv, who edited the rough original pieces, inserted insightful comments and encouraged me to always continue writing.

To Sam Merel, my new friend and unofficial editor who spent so much of her own time pouring over, refining and line editing the rough drafts.

To all my lay editors, my audiologist Maureen, the nurses in my OR, Fran especially, and my medical assistants Janis and Joan who tolerated my incessant discussion of this passion project and enthusiastically read countless bits and pieces of the unfinished manuscript.

To all my beloved friends and family who were part of my story, whether they made it into this book or not.

Endnotes

1   U.S. Breast Cancer Statistics. Retrieved from http://www.breast-cancer.org/symptoms/understand_bc/statistics

2   Oeffinger KC, Fontham ETH, Etzioni R, Herzig A, Michaelson JS, Shih YT, Walter LC, Church TR, Flowers CR, LaMonte SJ, Wolf AMD, DeSantis C, Lortet-Tieulent J, Andrews K, Manassaram-Baptiste D, Saslow D, Smith RA, Brawley OW, Wender R. Breast Cancer Screening for Women at Average Risk 2015 Guideline Update From the American Cancer Society. *JAMA.* 2015;314(15):1599–1614. doi:10.1001/jama.2015.12783

3   American Cancer Society Release New Breast Cancer Guideline. Retrieved from https://www.cancer.org/latest-news/america n-cancer-society-releases-new-breast-cancer-guidelines.html

4   Fisher B, Costantino JP, Redmond CK, Fisher ER, Wickerham DL, Cronin WM. Endometrial cancer in tamoxifen-treated breast cancer patients: findings from the National Surgical Adjuvant Breast and Bowel Project (NSABP) B-14. J Natl Cancer Inst 1994; 86:527–37.

5   Francis PA[1], Regan MM, Fleming GF, Láng I, Ciruelos E, Bellet M, Bonnefoi HR, Climent MA, Da Prada GA, Burstein HJ, Martino S, Davidson NE, Geyer CE Jr, Walley BA, Coleman R, Kerbrat P, Buchholz S, Ingle JN, Winer EP, Rabaglio-Poretti M, Maibach R, Ruepp B, Giobbie-Hurder A, Price KN, Colleoni M, Viale G, Coates AS, Goldhirsch A, Gelber RD; SOFT Investigators;

International Breast Cancer Study Group. Adjuvant ovarian suppression in premenopausal breast cancer. Engl J Med. 2015; 29;372(5):436-46.

6 Holy Bible, New International Version®, NIV® Copyright ©1973, 1978, 1984, 2011 by <u>Biblica, Inc.®</u> Used by permission. All rights reserved worldwide.

About the Author

Tali Lando Aronoff, M.D., is a full-time pediatric otolaryngology (ENT) surgeon with a busy practice split between her offices and the operating room. She is also a mother of three young girls and an enthusiastic scuba diver and breast cancer survivor. She grew up in Allentown, Pennsylvania, and lived in New York  City for a decade before settling in Westchester, New York, with her husband and children.

Made in the USA
Middletown, DE
08 November 2018